100 Innovative Ideas for Florida's Future

100 Innovative Ideas for Florida's Future

REGNERY
PUBLISHING, INC.
An Eagle Publishing Company • Since 1947

Cataloging-in-Publication data on file with the Library of Congress

ISBN 1-59698-511-9
ISBN 13 978-1-59698-511-7

Published in the United States by
Regnery Publishing, Inc.
One Massachusetts Avenue, NW
Washington, DC 20001
www.regnery.com

Distributed to the trade by
National Book Network
Lanham, MD 20706
Manufactured in the United States of America

10 9 8 7 6 5 4 3 2 1

Books are available in quantity for promotional or premium use. Write to Director of Special Sales, Regnery Publishing, Inc., One Massachusetts Avenue NW, Washington, DC 20001, for information on discounts and terms or call (202) 216-0600.

To the people of the State of Florida, whose ideas made this book possible.

All proceeds from the sale of this book will go toward providing academic scholarships to benefit the next generation of ideamakers.

TABLE OF CONTENTS

Foreword

Introduction

Chapter I: Learning, Growing, and Competing in the 21st Century

Student Learning—Preparing Our Students for the Global Marketplace

1. Enhance the value of the Florida Comprehensive Assessment Test (FCAT) by raising the curricular standards it measures and using its results to reward high performance.
2. Systematically and sequentially replace the Sunshine State Standards with a new, world-class curriculum comparable to those found in the leading education systems in the world.
3. Ensure student mastery of the appropriate knowledge at each grade level by developing statewide end-of-course examinations to match new, more challenging standards.
4. Begin administering the FCAT as late in the school year as possible with results still returned before the end of the school year.
5. Make Florida's Voluntary Pre-Kindergarten Program a global model for school readiness.
6. Encourage trained and certified curriculum leaders in reading, math, and science, and in the new curricular standards in every school.
7. Provide strong incentives to identify gifted elementary school children and require our elementary schools to allow these children to work at a suitably challenging academic level.

8. Provide our elementary school children with the advantages of learning a second language by encouraging and incentivizing a foreign language curriculum in all elementary schools.

9. Encourage the establishment of certified ninth grade success centers as "schools within a school."

10. Create career academies and career training programs that allow students to become industry certified in a technical field, both as part of and after their high school education.

11. Achieve America's best meaningful graduation rate by adding a new component to our accountability system's reward program—the School Recognition Program—that introduces additional rewards to high schools that achieve measured rising graduation rates based on test score outcomes.

12. Ensure the full implementation of policies relating to credit transfers, the expansion of articulation policies, and the elimination of any unnecessary barriers or impediments to postsecondary students.

13. Make public funding of universities contingent on university performance and outcomes.

14. Develop strategic fiscal policies that address the scope of each program for which state universities and community colleges will receive state support.

15. Commit to having a Top 10 public university in Florida.

World-Class Teachers and Principals Make World-Class Schools

16. Pay teachers and principals based on performance and merit.

17. Require the statewide development and delivery of improved professional development courses for teachers and principals—offered online, through virtual means, or by satellite/cable—that emphasize new curricular standards and have measurable outcomes based on both student assessment and teacher statewide competency tests.
18. Encourage collaboration among universities, businesses, education colleges, and specialty public-private partnerships to provide excellent principal preparation programs.
19. Create statewide competency tests based on new curricular standards for both new and veteran teachers at each grade level and subject area.
20. Fully certify any teacher who passes a background check and holds a bachelor's degree and demonstrates substantive competence by having the relevant college degree in a specified area, or by passing a rigorous test.
21. Increase the probationary period for teachers from three to five years.
22. Protect our teachers by insulating them from liability.
23. Consider piloting student-based funding programs.

Empowering Parents and Students

24. Continue to add options for student and parent choice in education.
25. Increase virtual schooling.
26. Identify professions in high demand that are currently experiencing shortages and provide incentives for students to remain in Florida and enter these professions.

School System Reforms

27. Provide voters with the option of dividing large school districts into smaller districts.
28. Create and fund an Inspector General or other watchdog to track specific incidents of fraud, waste, and abuse that occur each year in Florida public schools.
29. Require all schools that accept state funds, including community colleges and universities, to send parents annual notices delineating school content, performance, and spending.
30. Charge the Department of Education with annually evaluating the performance of the graduates of state-approved teacher preparation programs.
31. Streamline the traditional state-approved teacher preparation programs offered by colleges of education by revising mandatory, uniform core curricula and pre-service field experience requirements.
32. Provide incentives to create innovative public-private partnerships that will expand after-school programs.
33. Pursue public-private partnerships to provide classroom construction, leasing, maintenance, and school services.

Chapter II: Restoring Accountability and Delivering Results

Florida Government Accountability Act

34. Create and empower a Sunset Advisory Committee to increase the effectiveness of the review process of state agencies and programs.

Policy Choices Should Drive Budget Choices

35. Combine fiscal and substantive committees into a single committee that will develop and fund the most appropriate policy issues for Florida.
36. Design an e-budget website that will display a detailed, issue-level budget and allow the public to comment on the budget.

Securing Florida's Place on the National Stage

37. Move up the timing of Florida's presidential primary.

Protecting the Citizen Initiative Process from Special Interests

38. Enact legislation to reduce the growth of the paid petition business and the influence of moneyed special interests in the citizen initiative process.

Chapter III: Safe Homes, Safe Streets, Safe Communities

Life Without Exception for Sexual Predators

39. Expand the dangerous sexual felony offender law.
40. Expand DNA collection by 2012 to include all those convicted of felony offenses and those who have exhibited a propensity for sexually deviant behavior through commission of specified misdemeanor offenses.
41. Enact laws to deny registered sex offenders and stalkers access to popular Internet networking sites mostly used by

underage children and install tracking equipment on their computers to monitor their use.

Florida Anti-Pornography Plan
42. Increase the risk and penalties for those engaged in the business of promoting sex crimes.
43. Afford whistleblower status to everyone who reports sex crimes, even if they were involved in the act.

Gang/Hate Group Elimination
44. Increase funding for additional law enforcement resources to combat gang activities.
45. Increase the numbers of specialized prosecutors and gang-related law enforcement officers, and establish training programs for them to develop better methods to combat gang and hate group activity.

Curb Endless Appeals by Convicted Felons
46. Limit the time convicted felons have to appeal their sentences.

Chapter IV: Keep Florida Moving . . . Forward

Improving Florida's Roadways through Private Sector Involvement
47. Partner with private companies to build a model transportation system.
48. Lease existing toll roads to private companies.

Privatize the Division of Drivers' Licenses

49. Allow private companies to operate the Division of Drivers' Licenses.
50. Offer multiple-year vehicle registrations.

Protection from Identity Theft

51. Enhance penalties for identity theft crimes that affect persons sixty-five years or older.
52. Make any unauthorized possession of another's personal identity information a felony.
53. Adopt an "opt in" policy that requires government and business to receive permission from citizens before distributing any of their personal information.

Affordable Homeowners' Insurance for Florida

54. Increase funding of home inspections and grants to upgrade homes to better withstand hurricanes by creating a recurring source of funding.
55. Ensure all insurance companies provide appropriate, easily understood credits or discounts to homeowners engaging in hurricane mitigation.
56. Consider adopting a uniform grading system for evaluating the hurricane strength of homes, allowing homeowners to become insured by the private market or to take full and appropriate advantage of the measures undertaken to fortify their homes.
57. Adopt a uniform statewide building code.
58. Allow the Florida Hurricane Catastrophe Fund to give companies the option to buy

more reinsurance from the fund below the current retention and charge near-market rates.

59. Allow insurers to offer all homeowners policies with higher hurricane deductibles.

60. Permit policyholders to reduce their hurricane deductible if they implement meaningful and verifiable mitigation measures.

61. Create a comprehensive package of consumer protections that should include, among other provisions, requiring a "Truth in Premium Billing" statement delineating the various components and prices of changes in premiums.

62. Ensure that insurance companies expedite payments for damages and consider expanding the short-term, no-interest bridge loan program.

63. Advocate for the federal government to establish a Federal Natural Catastrophe Reinsurance Fund, allow insurers to accumulate tax-deferred reserves for catastrophes, and create "Hurricane Savings Accounts."

Chapter V: Putting Families First

Improved Access to Affordable Housing

64. Increase incentives for developers to not only provide the land for affordable housing, but also construct the housing units themselves.

Protecting Florida's Children

> 65. Limit the number of passengers who can be transported by drivers age eighteen and under.
> 66. Require social networking sites to set up verification systems to require parental notification and consent for minors to use these sites.
> 67. Require schools to include in their codes of conduct clear instructions to students about what information is acceptable to post on social networking websites.

Localize and Streamline the Department of Children and Families

> 68. Enhance independence and flexibility for community-based care.
> 69. Create a statutory mechanism for communities to create "Children's Zones."

Chapter VI: A Cleaner, Safer, Healthier Florida

Energy-Efficient Buildings Reward Program

> 70. Implement a voluntary statewide incentive program for energy efficiency.
> 71. Create an Energy Efficiency Fund to offer loans to public schools, public hospitals, cities, counties, special districts, and public care institutions.
> 72. Provide tax incentives to encourage homeowners and businesses to purchase energy-efficient appliances and systems.
> 73. Build energy-efficient buildings.

Environmental "Gold Star" Recognition

74. Create a performance-based permitting program that rewards top environmental performers.

Promote the Development of Alternative Energy Sources

75. Foster the development and use of alternative energy sources and ethanol production.

Fuel-Efficient Vehicle Reward Program

76. Offer additional incentives for clean alternative-fueled vehicles and hybrid passenger vehicles.
77. Convert state government vehicles into a high fuel efficiency fleet.

Chapter VII: Quality Healthcare at an Affordable Price

Expanded Choice in Medicaid

78. Give Medicaid participants control over their own health while encouraging healthy habits.

Value-Based Financial Support for Florida's Hospitals

79. Secure accountability for quality and costs from hospitals receiving tax support.
80. Improve efficiency and performance at state-owned and operated hospitals by evaluating outsourcing and other potential operational changes.

Coordinated Care for Florida's Seniors

81. Implement Florida Senior Care to allow Florida seniors to remain independent and receive the care they need at home and in their communities.

Use Transparency to Foster Value-Based Healthcare Decisions

82. Reward healthcare providers and plans that demonstrate better outcomes at lower cost.

83. Create a "one-stop" source of information on assistance for Florida's uninsured.

84. Reward physicians who use technology like e-prescribing to reduce errors and improve efficiency.

85. Improve patient care through technology by expanding electronic health records and regional health information networks.

Accountable, Accessible Healthcare

86. Make it easier for qualified, uninsured children to get coverage through Florida KidCare.

87. Launch a marketplace of affordable health insurance.

88. Encourage healthcare providers to expand preventive services and walk-in care for uninsured Floridians.

89. Help hospitals serve patients with immediate medical problems to avoid emergency departments while still receiving the necessary care.

Chapter VIII: Opportunity and Prosperity for the Next Generation

Create a Family-Friendly Hollywood in Florida

90. Create a tax incentive program aimed at attracting more film production and TV series to the state.

Business Development

91. Establish a nationally recognized business investment program to encourage creation of more high-wage jobs for Floridians.

Loser Pays for Frivolous Lawsuits

92. Expand the "loser pays" or "prevailing party" attorneys' fee statutes, strengthen the "offer of judgment" statute, and ensure that any case, claim, or defense not supported by necessary facts or law results in the right to claim attorneys' fees.

Give Citizens Greater Control over Government Taxing and Spending Policies

93. Adopt a constitutional amendment prohibiting Florida governments from growing faster than the incomes of their taxpaying citizens.
94. Require a supermajority vote for any tax increases.
95. Reduce the tax on phone, cable, cellular, and satellite services.

Constitutionally Eliminate or Cap Skyrocketing Property Taxes

96. Amend the Florida Constitution to either place caps on all property taxes or,

alternatively, abolish the property tax in whole or in part.

Standardized Business Courts
97. Establish a business specialty court.

Economic Civil Rights for Communities
98. Institute a pilot program that creates a tax-free zone in Florida's most economically depressed areas.
99. Establish Housing First as an alternative to the prevalent system of emergency shelter/transitional housing.

National Idea Bank
100. Create a nationwide web-based "Idea Bank" that documents programs and initiatives that have succeeded.

Acknowledgments
Index

Foreword

For the better part of 160 years, Floridians have proven that the pioneer spirit is alive and well—and still one of our core cultural values. We are a people who readily see the sunlight through the clouds, and count every day as an opportunity to change the world.

Floridians have bravely faced the rigors of our paradise: wildfires, alligators, mosquitoes, hard freezes, fruit flies, flash floods, citrus canker, and, of course, hurricanes. But we still enjoy our sunrises and sunsets. We are quick to help a neighbor in need, and reluctant to take "no" for an answer. We still gaze in awe at the sight of a space shuttle launch, and welcome tourists with open arms.

We have made the most of our cultural quilt: from a domino game on Little Havana's Calle Ocho to Friday night football in a Panhandle county seat. In our diversity, we are distinctly Floridian.

The 100 ideas contained in this book reflect the thoughts of thousands of Floridians who have taken time over the past year to offer their personal insight into what it will take to preserve our state's legacy of opportunity. In countless idearaisers, forward-thinking citizens have dropped ideas in the basket. Some call for systemic change. Others refine earlier reforms. But the tie that binds them all together is the belief that ascendancy is only possible when complacency is eradicated.

Florida's firm foundation is not built on misgivings and hesitation. Nor will the decisions made for her future. This book will challenge the traditional thinkers who continue to rely on government for satisfaction. All great movements in history—and especially in Florida—withstood the rigors of the critics, the disdain of those protecting the status quo, and the notion that all good ideas originate only from the tip of government's pen.

Over the past eight years, I have repeatedly faced two choices: either tinker with systems clearly not working, and rest on the laurels of having made a bad system a little less bad; or dive headlong into debates that would attract the critics, risk being ridiculed, and maybe, just maybe, transform the system. I chose the latter.

Whether it was the A+ Plan for Education and its successor reforms, One Florida for diversity in government procurement and university admissions, the new Medicaid recently embarked on, or 10/20/Life, critics of change often fanned the flames of fear and folly. Nonetheless, we stuck to our guns, and time is proving us right. Children are learning because we dared to measure and hold schools accountable. Underserved segments of our population are being empowered because we have given the tools to succeed. Our streets are safer because criminals are being locked up.

In life, progress results from a marriage of good ideas and the courage to see those ideas through. That is why the ideas in this book are so promising.

In the fall of 2005 at a House Republican Conference ceremony, I recall listening with bated breath as a young Cuban-American legislator persuasively made the case for this book. On that day, he opened the book to display its curiously blank pages, emphasizing that the ideas for Florida's future would be written with the input of Floridians. He struck a noticeable chord that continues to resound.

I commend House Speaker-Designate Marco Rubio for his effort to infuse the dialogue of real Floridians into the policy arena. We share a belief that the immigrant small business owner in Miami and the healthcare worker in Cape Coral should have a seat at the table when decisions are made that shape their state's future. From schoolteachers in Pensacola to citrus growers in Sebring, he has enlisted his fellow citizens in an initiative that you will see reflected in the pages of this treatise. No longer blank—the book is filled with the energy of ideas!

I challenge the legislators and leaders of Florida to make this a reference guide for transforming the political landscape. Don't allow this book to sit silently on a shelf or gather dust on a table. Bring the ideas contained herein to life, impact the future, and let the pioneering voices of Florida be heard.

Do not let the bold ideas that leap from your heart fall silent on your lips because you fear they are unpopular. Give life and legitimacy to innovative notions by adjoining yourself to noble initiatives, not upcoming elections.

I challenge my fellow Floridians to consider their place in public service. One need not stand for election or sit in a legislative chamber in order to affect good government. With my term of public office nearing completion, I, too, will soon find myself living and working as a private citizen—but that does not excuse me from my obligation to society.

Each and every one of us has a role. For good or for bad, government affects our daily lives. Its success rises and falls on the attention and scrutiny we afford to its maintenance. Let the public become disengaged and unconcerned, and government will cater to itself. But let people become vocal and vigorous about its decisions, and government will have to respond.

Resolve to make these the *first* 100 ideas—with thousands more to come. Make your voice known at the ballot box, in public forums, on the editorial page, and through civic involvement. Dare to dream, but never doubt, that the world is at Florida's fingertips and the potential to reach out and secure tomorrow can be found today—*in your ideas!*

Governor Jeb Bush
Tallahassee, Florida

Introduction

In September of 2005, we embarked on an effort to connect with the people of our state. We asked them a simple question. If they were in our position, in the state legislature, what would they do? Their answers will forever change the way we approach politics in Florida, and hopefully America.

Their answers gave us insight on what families all across Florida are talking about at their dinner tables. It put us at the office water cooler, where co-workers share their hopes and fears with one another.

We heard many expected concerns. Education, healthcare, and the rising cost of living are on everyone's mind. But it was those issues we never heard discussed in the capital, but kept coming up everywhere we went, that taught us the biggest lessons.

Today's modern political process is reactive. It reacts to a crisis that causes great damage. It reacts to a media exposé of a wrong that needs to be corrected. And it reacts to special interests that spend countless hours and millions of dollars to influence the process.

No matter how common a concern may be, it is not usually addressed by the modern political process until it becomes a crisis, is exposed by the media, or you hire someone to lobby on your behalf.

We need to change that. Politics needs to become more proactive. Tomorrow's crises are only emerging problems today, and it is easier and less expensive to solve them now. But when problems go unresolved for too long, they become a crisis. Then the options narrow, and the price goes up.

100 Innovative Ideas for Florida's Future is our best effort to make politics proactive, to harness the incredible wisdom of everyday people, and to connect politics with people's everyday lives.

The search for good ideas should be a never-ending process. Our hope is that many of these 100 ideas will be replaced with even better ones. Some of our ideas can be accomplished quickly. Others will take months, even years. Through my partnership with Speakers Ray Sansom and Dean Cannon, we will spend the next six years striving to move them forward. If we can make politics about ideas again, we can begin to solve many of our most difficult problems, and thus avoid the crisis of tomorrow.

Those of us in politics have a tendency to talk. What we need to do is strengthen our commitment to listen. Listen to the people we serve. In their voices and in their lives, in their fears and in their hopes, you will find the challenges of today, and the promise of tomorrow.

Speaker Marco Rubio

Learning, Growing, and Competing in the 21st Century

IDEAS

1-15

> *"Success is never final, and reform is never finished."*   Jeb Bush, 2006

Student Learning— Preparing Our Students for the Global Marketplace

Problem: The public education system needs continued reform.

Improving education in Florida means acting differently than we have in the past. It means transformation. Concepts we accept as proven principles of performance—that competition improves the quality of service and products; people achieve more when held accountable for results and rewarded for success; and commitment to quality in the workforce—all seem to be difficult concepts to apply to our education system.

In 1999, we rocked Florida's K–12 education world by enacting the "A+ plan for education," a bold and revolutionary program based on high standards and expectations, clear measurement and accountability, and rewards and consequences for results. This was only our starting point, and since then we have embarked on the largest effort of all fifty states to implement policies, practices, and funding initiatives to improve classroom reading abilities. We significantly expanded education choice options by way of charter schools, virtual schools, and path-breaking scholarship programs. We have accomplished so much, but there is still more to be done.

Graduation Rate

Florida counts every student, and the graduation rate is increasing.

Before A+ Plan	Now
1999	2005
60.2% of all students	71.9% of all students
52.8% of Hispanic students	64.5% of Hispanic students
48.7% of African American students	57.1% of African American students

Dropout Rate

Fewer Florida students are dropping out, and the decline is led by minority students.

Before A+ Plan	Now
1999	2005
5.4% of all students	3.0% of all students
8.3% of Hispanic students	3.6% of Hispanic students
6.6% of African American students	3.9% of African American students

Choice Programs

Florida's choice options include three K–12 scholarship programs that are the largest in the nation, a charter school enrollment that is the second highest in the nation, and the nation's first statewide public virtual school that is a nationally recognized e-learning mode.

Before A+ Plan	Now
2001	2006
Opportunity Scholarships: 51	Opportunity Scholarships: 734
McKay Scholarships: 970	McKay Scholarships: 17,300
Corporate Tax Credit Scholarships: 15,585 (2002–2003)	Corporate Tax Credit Scholarships: 14.061
1999	2005
Charter School Students: 9,135	Charter School Students: 92,214
Virtual school half-credit course enrollments: 1,100	Virtual school half-credit course enrollments: 68,000

Bright Futures Funding

There has been a dramatic increase in funding and the number of awards for Bright Futures scholarships in Florida since its inception in 1997.

Before A+ Plan	Now
1999	2005
$93,332,570 FY 1998–99	$346,342,906 FY 2006–07
56,065 awards in 1998–99	149,389 (estimated) awards in 2006–07

Community Colleges

Nearly half of Florida's community colleges rank in the nation's top 100 (based on the number of associate degrees awarded). Four of Florida's community colleges are in the top 10.

Before A+ Plan	Now
1999	2005
716,228 students enrolled	749,690 students enrolled (up 5%)
25,720 earned Associated in Arts (AA) degrees	33,398 earned Associate in Arts (AA) degrees (up 30%)
1999	2005
17,369 community college students in 1998 were found in the state university system in 1999	20,407 community college students in 2004 were found in the state university system in 2005 (up 17%)

University Enrollment

Under One Florida, more minorities are coming to Florida's public universities without the use of racial quotas.

Before A+ Plan	Now
1999	2005
36% of university freshmen were minority	39% of university freshmen were minority
21% of new graduate students were minority	24% of new graduate students were minority
24% of new law students were minority	34% of new law students were minority
32% of all students were minority	35% of all students were minority

SCHOOL GRADES

Florida has seen a dramatic increase in school grades, even after raising the bar in 2001 and again in 2004.

	Before A+ Plan	Now
School Grade	1999	2006
A	202	1,467
B	313	610
C	1,230	570
D	601	121
F	76	21

FLORIDA COMPREHENSIVE ASSESSMENT TEST (FCAT)

More students are reading on grade level and Florida is closing the achievement gap.

4th Grade Students Reading On or Above Grade Level	
Before A+ Plan	Now
1999	2006
51% of all students	66% of all students
37% of Hispanics	60% of Hispanics
23% of African Americans	49% of African Americans

NATIONAL ASSESSMENT OF EDUCATIONAL PROGRESS (NAEP—"THE NATION'S REPORT CARD")

The percent of Florida 4th grade students proficient in reading has increased 29 percentage points since 1988—from 15 percent to 44 percent. The percent of Florida 4th grade students proficient in mathematics has increased by 33 percentage points since 1998—from 22 percent to 52 percent.

4th Grade Reading	
Before A+ Plan	Now
1998	2005
Median scale score: 206	Median scale score: 219
Median for Hispanic students: 198	Median for Hispanic students: 215
Median for African American students: 186	Median for African American students: 203
4th Grade Writing	
1998	2002
Florida did not participate	Florida 4th graders ranked 8th in the nation
	Hispanic 4th graders ranked 3rd in the nation

SAT

More graduates and more minority students are taking the SAT.

Before A+ Plan	Now
1999	2006
56% of gradautes took the SAT, or 62,524 students	63% of graduates took the SAT, or 94,601 students
39% of test takers were minority	44% of test takers were minority
Combined score: 997	Combined score: 993

SCHOOL RECOGNITION

Florida has seen a dramatic increase in the number of schools receiving school recognition funds, which requires schools to earn a grade of A or increase school grade by at least one letter grade.

Before A+ Plan	Now
1999	2006
319 schools shared $27,603,881	1,799 schools shared $157,587,811

PSAT

More students are taking the PSAT in Florida and Florida leads the nation in minority test takers. Through a partnership with the College Board, Florida offers the PSAT free of charge to all Florida 10th grade students.

Before A+ Plan	Now
Fall 1998*	Fall 2005*
33,522 total 10th grade test takers	141,685 total 10th grade test takers
4,655 10th grade Hispanic test takers	35,112 10th grade Hispanic test takers
3,436 10th grade African American test takers	27,566 10th grade African American test takers
*Fall 1998 includes PSAT given to 10th grade students in both public and nonpublic schools. Separate PSAT information for public schools only is not available before 1999.	*Fall 2005 includes PSAT given to 10th grade students in public schools only.

ADVANCED PLACEMENT (AP)

In Florida, the increase in number of test takers since 1998 is more than twice the national increase.

Before A+ Plan	Now
1999	2005
34,607 AP test takers	90,661 AP test takers (up 162%)
6,181 Hispanic AP test takers	20,421 Hispanic AP test takers (up 230%)
2,595 African American AP test takers	8,788 African American AP test takers (up 239%)

Florida's most vital resource is its children. Our priority must be to overcome the status quo of our education system and to prepare students to successfully compete in the world economy. Our students are growing up in a new era. They no longer compete only against students from Georgia or

Our students must be equipped to compete in a world economy.

Louisiana. They compete globally against students from China, India, and Singapore—students who strive toward the highest standards possible and are subjected to the most rigorous curricula. Their middle school students master our high school algebra and geometry while ours are mired in arithmetic. Their middle school students discuss the world's great works of literature while ours read adolescent stories.

Large-scale reforms require long-term commitment. It took a generation of school decline to metastasize into today's problems, and it will take at least half that long, pursuing a consistent vision of transformation, to fix them. It is the cumulative pressure of constant incremental improvement that creates significant progress.

In 2006, we built on the A+ legislation of 1999 by passing the A++ bill, which implemented major middle and high school reforms. Success in middle school requires a strong foundation of knowledge and skills developed in the elementary grades, and achievement in high school likewise demands comprehensive abilities built in the elementary and middle school years. Our 2006 high school reforms will begin with the 2007–2008 school year and will include a new emphasis not only on academic rigor but on context and relevance to our students' real lives and futures. If we have the courage to impose transformational reform on our entire curricular framework, our new reforms will revolutionize the entire educational experience of Florida's students, providing them with paths to great careers.

We need to add a multiplicity of career academy options and create a variety of great career academies in which students can focus on math and science, fine arts, or career and technical skills, depending on their goals and interests. The objective is for students to graduate with career goals and the skills to achieve them. They can leave school armed with college credits, or, if they choose a vocational route, with certified skills for a specific industry. Students who can see the relationship between their classes and their dreams are more likely to stay focused and stay in school. They should leave school industry-certified and ready for the world of work, postsecondary education, or both.

Florida students will define and determine the future of our state. If we get education right, all other issues become easier—from fostering strong economic development to strengthening the social fabric and laying the cornerstone of American democracy that binds our communities together and strengthens our nation.

> **Solution: Transform Florida's education from pre-kindergarten through postsecondary while continually building upon the foundation we began in 1999.**

Our statewide idearaisers resulted in numerous practical ideas for transforming our education system. First, we should <u>enhance the value of the Florida Comprehensive Assessment Test (FCAT)</u> by

IDEA
1

raising the curricular standards it measures and using its results to reward high performance. The FCAT is the core accountability tool of the A+ Plan for Education. Student FCAT performance is the basis for schools' evaluations as well as monetary rewards for teachers and schools. It is the measurement tool educators and policymakers use to determine whether students are making progress in reading, writing, math, and science. The FCAT must be based on truly rigorous academic standards if Florida is to achieve a first-class school system.

Strong incentives should be provided to students to encourage high FCAT performance. For example, high FCAT scores could make students eligible for a Bright Futures Scholarship or exempt them from the Common Placement Test for community college credit courses. Florida colleges and universities could consider FCAT scores in evaluating college preparedness or offering prioritized entrance. High FCAT scores in the tenth grade could allow for creating an early college environment for high school students. Further, as we raise the bar, we must add eleventh and twelfth grade examinations. By rewarding high FCAT performance, Florida will be encouraging individual responsibility and educational accountability. A reasonable reward system for students is a step toward our ultimate goal—to provide a quality education for every student. We must continue clearly and positively to send the message that in Florida, responsibility is prized, achievement rewarded, and ever-higher expectations demanded.

The FCAT measures our students' competency on our Sunshine State Standards. These standards must be revised, made more rigorous, and encompass more areas of study. This is an opportunity to align Florida's curricular standards with the best in the world. Why should Florida's math standards be inferior to

Singapore's? Why should Florida's reading standards lag behind Finland's? The answer is, of course, that they should not.

How the U.S. Stacks Up

SCIENCE	MATH	READING
Average combined science literacy scores of 15-year-old students, PISA results	Average combined math literacy scores of 15-year-old students, PISA results	Average combined reading literacy scores of 15-year-old students, 2003 PISA results

Country	Score	Country	Score	Country	Score
Finland	548	Hong Kong ✪	550	Finland	543
Japan	548	Finland	544	Korea	534
Hong Kong	539	Korea	542	Canada	528
Korea	538	Netherlands	538	Australia	525
Liechtenstein	525	Liechtenstein	536	Liechtenstein	525
Australia	525	Japan	534	New Zealand	522
Macao	525	Canada	532	Ireland	515
Netherlands	524	Belgium	529	Sweden	514
Czech Republic	523	Macao	527	Netherlands	513
New Zealand	521	Switzerland	527	Hong Kong	510
Canada	519	Australia	524	Belgium	507
Switzerland	513	New Zealand	523	Norway	500
France	511	Czech Republic	516	Switzerland	499
Belgium	509	Iceland	515	Japan	498
Sweden	506	Denmark	514	Macao	498
Ireland	505	France	511	Poland	497
Hungary	503	Sweden	509	France	496
Germany	502	Austria	506	**United States**	**495**
Poland	498	Germany	503	Denmark	492
Slovak Republic	495	Ireland	503	Iceland	492
Iceland	495	Slovak Republic	498	Germany	491
United States	**491**	Norway	495	Austria	491
Austria	491	Luxembourg	493	Latvia	491
Russia	489	Poland	490	Czech Republic	489
Latvia	489	Hungary	490	Hungary	482
Spain	487	Spain	485	Spain	481
Italy	486	Latvia	483	Luxembourg	479
Norway	484	**United States**	**483**	Portugal	478
Luxembourg	483	Russia	468	Italy	476
Greece	481	Portugal	466	Greece	472
Denmark	475	Italy	466	Slovak Republic	469
Portugal	468	Greece	445	Russia	442
Uruguay	438	Serbia	437	Turkey	441
Serbia	436	Turkey	423	Uruguay	434
Turkey	434	Uruguay	422	Thailand	420
Thailand	429	Thailand	417	Serbia	412
Mexico	405	Mexico	385	Brazil	403
Indonesia	395	Indonesia	360	Mexico	400
Brazil	390	Tunisia	359	Indonesia	382
Tunisia	385	Brazil	356	Tunisia	375

✪ On TIMSS rankings, Singapore scores first among all countries and Hong Kong scores third.

The Florida Legislature will accept no less than the best curricular standards and instructional materials that the top countries in the world have for their students. We will not lose another generation of Florida students to mediocrity. We will demand detailed, sequenced, content-oriented core reading, math, and science curricular standards and industry-driven technical content that build from grade to grade throughout our K–12 system and beyond in order to keep our students competitive in the worldwide arena. We will reevaluate our instructional material adoption process and accept no less than top-quality materials that meet our new curricular standards. According to the new Koret Task Force report, *Reforming Education in Florida*, "If Florida revamps its curriculum as it implements the changes in state standards so as to ensure a steady acquisition of essential knowledge...it can become a pioneer in curricular reform, just as it has been one in accountability and school choice." Therefore, we will systematically and sequentially replace the Sunshine State Standards with a new, world-class curriculum comparable to those found in the leading education systems in the world. We will strive to have the strongest, deepest, and best-aligned curricular standards in the world. With these world-class standards in place, future Florida kindergartners will rank in the top 5 percent of the world's students when they graduate from high school.

Additionally, as part of our new curriculum framework, we will ensure student mastery of the appropriate knowledge at each grade level by developing statewide end-of-course examinations to match the new standards. Exams in Algebra II and eleventh grade English will include those standards indicating readiness for college.

IDEA 2

IDEA 3

To help maximize student achievement, Florida should continue to <u>push the administration of the FCAT as late in the school year as possible with results still returned before the end of the school year.</u> The FCAT is currently administered in early March to enable the release of scores to students, parents, and teachers before the end of the school year. By improving the FCAT format and implementing appropriate technological advances, we can have the exam administered later. This should improve overall student achievement by giving students the widest possible window for learning and the quickest feedback about areas of improvement.

IDEA
4

A critical foundation for learning includes a strong preschool program focused on developing literacy and numeracy. According to the Koret Task Force Report, "With the major expansion of its preschool program now under way, Florida has the potential to be a national leader in this regard." The Koret Task Force Report praises Florida's new voluntary pre-kindergarten program for its features of decentralization, independence from public schools, wide variety of choice options, strong literacy standards, results-based system of measurement, provider participation, and realistic structure. <u>Florida's voluntary pre-kindergarten program can become a global model for school readiness.</u> This can be accomplished by:

IDEA
5

1. Developing a data system for the program that is comparable to the current data system for our K–12 education system and stimulating careful research on the best ways to measure the program's educational impact.

2. Reevaluating the governance structure to ensure efficiency and accountability.

3. Removing any participation obstacles for those students in most need of these services.

To ensure Florida's children can take full advantage of the opportunities our education system offers, Florida will <u>encourage trained and certified curriculum leaders in reading, math, and science, and in the new curricular standards in every school.</u> With these strong curriculum leaders in place and leading each of our schools with a well-defined, world-class K–12 curriculum in the major areas of study, we will establish the powerful foundation essential to successful student achievement in elementary school, middle school, and high school.

As Florida's population increases and becomes more diverse, we must enhance the education of our elementary school children. In addition to the new detailed, sequenced, content-oriented, grade-to-grade core curricular standards, two major initiatives will help these students. First, we will <u>provide strong incentives to identify gifted elementary school children and require our elementary schools to allow these children to work at a suitably challenging academic level</u> and progress at the pace of their own potential. Thus, a third-grader who can read tenth grade material or a fourth-grader who can do eighth grade math should be given those challenges.

Secondly, we will <u>provide our elementary school children with the advantages of learning a second language by encouraging and incentivizing a foreign language curriculum in all elementary schools.</u> Schools choosing to offer more than one foreign language would be assisted with the necessary resources. Foreign language is already included as a critical needs area, and additional incentives can be offered to teachers to encourage them to staff these programs. Aside from the obvious educational advantage, widespread elementary foreign language education offers long-term economic benefits. Over time, a multilingual school system will translate into a more knowledgeable workforce. An increasingly erudite society will increase

Florida's standard of living. The benefits of a multilingual education and dedication to better-educated students will change Florida's future and set a nationwide precedent.

To ease the difficult transition from middle school to high school and to reduce dropout rates, we will encourage the establishment of certified ninth grade success centers as "schools within a school." These self-contained centers, with their own administrative and interdisciplinary teaching staff, strongly impact the education of participating fourteen-year-olds and are demonstrably effective in lowering dropout rates. The ninth graders in these success centers must be shown articulated opportunities to attend technical college, both through technical dual enrollment opportunities and post-graduation opportunities. Strong ninth grade success centers serve as a bridge over the rough waters of adolescence, preparing young adolescents academically and socially for the rigors of high school, postsecondary education, and successful careers.

IDEA 9

To further modernize Florida's education system, we must further expand the middle school magnet programs and high school and postsecondary career academies that are the cornerstone of this transformation. Therefore, Florida should create career academies and career training programs that allow students to become industry certified in a technical field, both as part of and after their high school education. These will be programs that lead to successful employment in the growing Florida and world economies. One of the primary objectives of wide-ranging career and technical programs is to remove the negative stigma long associated with technical education. We have unwittingly created a culture that provides incentives for college educational progress while stigmatizing technical career paths. High skill and technological fields are understaffed

IDEA 10

as a result of inadequate options and career training at the middle school, high school, and postsecondary levels.

Career training reinforces Florida's commitment to educational choice for students and parents. After all, our ultimate goal is to provide an educational environment that allows *all* children to succeed. Through the growth of nationally certified career academies, industry-driven career and technical programs, district technical and career centers, and technical colleges, Florida can bolster its workforce and provide excellent employment opportunities to children who may have otherwise been lost in the system.

Key Facts – Student Demand

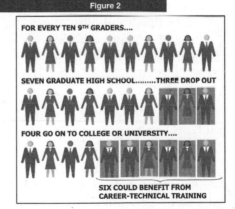

Figure 2

- Career education programs play a pivotal role in meeting the needs of the 6 out of 10 9th graders who drop out or do not enter immediately into college or university programs.

FOR EVERY TEN 9TH GRADERS....

SEVEN GRADUATE HIGH SCHOOL.........THREE DROP OUT

FOUR GO ON TO COLLEGE OR UNIVERSITY....

SIX COULD BENEFIT FROM CAREER-TECHNICAL TRAINING

Florida's graduation rate has improved from 60.2 percent in 1998–99 to 71.9 percent in 2004–05, but this is not good enough because it means we still have too many kids who are falling through the cracks. We will aim to <u>achieve America's best meaningful graduation rate by adding a new component to our accountability system's reward program—the School Recognition Program—that introduces additional rewards to high schools that achieve measured rising graduation rates based on test score outcomes.</u>

IDEA
11

To guarantee a better and more capable postgraduate labor force, Florida will institutionalize the certifications for high schoolers in certain occupations. Instead of pursuing separate state licensing after completion of a degree program, students will earn certification as part of their education. Upon graduation, students will be prepared for their chosen career without additional testing requirements.

Creating multiple certified career academy options and making certification and testing part of the curriculum will streamline the entrance of professionals into their fields. This is another way to reward students for their success. Both the state and its students will benefit. Florida will be committed to student progress, not bureaucratic process.

District technical/career centers, public community colleges, and state universities benefit Florida's citizens by providing access to affordable postsecondary educational opportunities and stimulating and expanding the state's economic development. It is the role of the Legislature to establish policies that maximize opportunities for postsecondary educational access and economic development while controlling costs to the taxpayer. An innovative program in Manatee County provides an instructive example of the benefits of cooperation among technical and educational institutions:

After Dr. Jay Schrock was hired as the Director of the School of Hospitality at Sarasota/Manatee University of South Florida, he sought to create a world-class school filled with eager future leaders of the hospitality industry. Lacking programs to help supply him with students, Dr. Schrock created a "2+2+2 agreement" with Manatee Community College and Manatee Technical Institute. This scheme allowed graduates of MTI's Culinary Arts Program to articulate their program at MCC, graduates of MCC's to articulate to the USF School of Hospitality, and MTI program participants—after four years in the program—to earn a Bachelor's in Applied Science with an emphasis in Hospitality Management at USF.

Since implementing this agreement in October 2005, enrollment in the Culinary Arts Program has increased every term. According to one MTI official, "Parents want their children to 'go to college,' and this articulated program enables parents to see their children on track for a Bachelor's within four years."

Florida has attempted to control costs and expand access to postsecondary education in many ways. Florida's open admissions policy provides high school students access to the state's community colleges. Florida's statewide articulation agreement facilitates the transition of students from secondary to postsecondary education—that is, from high school to a postsecondary career center or community college and on to a state university. The articulation agreement recognizes a variety of acceleration mechanisms, including dual enrollment, that provide opportunities for high school students—public and private and home-schooled—to earn post-secondary credit at little or no cost to students or their families. Florida's 2+2 system promotes our public community colleges as the primary point of entry for an undergraduate education, while the statewide articulation agreement guarantees community college graduates who receive an associate of arts degree admission to a state university. By providing many students with affordable access to an undergraduate education, the 2+2 policy reduces the enrollment pressures on state universities for the first two years of an undergraduate program. The statewide articulation agreement also guarantees the articulation of workforce programs between school districts and community colleges, as well as the articulation of appropriate courses within an associate of science program into a baccalaureate program.

Additionally, the statewide course numbering system facilitates student acceleration and the transfer of students and credits between school districts, public postsecondary educational institutions, and participating nonpublic postsecondary educational institutions by requiring the transfer and acceptance of credit for equivalent courses and among participating institutions. The Legislature will <u>ensure the full implementation of these policies, the expansion of existing programs that promote articulation policies, and the elimination of any unnecessary barriers or impediments to students in postsecondary educational programs</u> so that we can replicate programs like Manatee's throughout the state.

IDEA
12

Education and Training Pay...

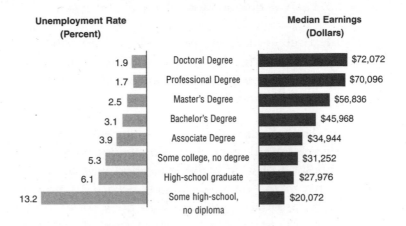

Unemployment Rate (Percent)		Median Earnings (Dollars)
1.9	Doctoral Degree	$72,072
1.7	Professional Degree	$70,096
2.5	Master's Degree	$56,836
3.1	Bachelor's Degree	$45,968
3.9	Associate Degree	$34,944
5.3	Some college, no degree	$31,252
6.1	High-school graduate	$27,976
13.2	Some high-school, no diploma	$20,072

Sources: Unemployment rate, 2004 annual average: Bureau of Labor Statistics;
Weekly Median Earnings (multiplied by 52 weeks), March 2004: Bureau of the Census.

When our students see the connection between their education and training and their future lives, they will strive for success.

In his book *The Costs of Higher Education*, Howard Bowen describes five laws that govern higher education costs:

1. The dominant goals of institutions are excellence, prestige, and influence.

2. In a quest for excellence, prestige, and influence, there is virtually no limit to the amount of money an institution could spend for seemingly fruitful educational ends. Once approved, expenditures

become long-term commitments from which it is difficult to withdraw.

3. Each institution raises all the money it can.

4. Each institution spends all it raises. The few institutions that become very affluent are able to save substantial amounts and accumulate significant endowments.

5. The cumulative effect of the preceding four laws leads toward ever increasing expenditures. The question of what higher education *ought* to cost—what is the minimal amount needed to provide services of acceptable quality—does not enter the process except when imposed from the outside. The higher educational system itself does not measure costs and benefits in terms of the public interest. The duty of setting limits thus falls—by default—upon those who provide the money, mostly legislators, students, and students' families.

These five points make clear our obligation as legislators to demand and protect a postsecondary education system that is academically and fiscally accountable to our students and their families. The Legislature has done a great deal to provide access for students by enacting policies that encourage articulation and acceleration; by creating statewide financial aid programs such as the Bright Futures Scholarship Program, the Florida Student Assistance Grant, and the First Generation Matching Grant Program; and by creating programs that help families plan for their children's education such as the Prepaid College Program and the College Savings Program. Now the universities must do their part. Funding will depend on university performance and outcomes, including but not limited to a thorough

IDEA

13

<u>review of university completion rates, the types of graduates produced, minority graduation rates, faculty contact, and guidance for students toward a clear path to complete their degrees.</u>

All of the state universities aspire to attain "flagship status" in a variety of programs in hopes of achieving national and international recognition. Community colleges, meanwhile, seek to award baccalaureate degrees when other alternatives may suffice at a lower cost to the taxpayer. We will <u>develop strategic fiscal policies that address the scope of each program for which state universities and community colleges will receive state support.</u> These policies aim to enhance the effectiveness of these programs, reduce unnecessary duplication, and maximize the return on investment to our citizens from this support. If the Legislature fails to do so, program proliferation is certain to proceed unabated at a great cost to the taxpayers of the State.

Florida should also seriously consider restructuring its post-secondary education system. One possible alternative is a three-tier system similar to California's: one tier would be the state's research institutions; a second tier would comprise numerous regional universities geared toward four-year degree programs; and a third tier would incorporate our system of community colleges.

Moreover, Florida should <u>commit to having a Top 10 public university.</u> Among the ten largest states, only Florida, Texas, and Ohio lack a Top 10 public or private university. Florida has the opportunity to move at least one of our state universities to national flagship status by enacting fiscal policies encouraging our high-ranking universities to be more competitive among their national peers. Because a rising tide raises all ships, national recognition of one or more of Florida's universities will help propel some of our other great universities into the Top 100 nationally, as has occurred in states like California. Our other state universities will also be supported as they seek to attain greater recognition at the national level in their respective areas of specialty or strength.

"It is the supreme art of the teacher to awaken joy in creative expression and knowledge." Albert Einstein

World-Class Teachers and Principals Make World-Class Schools

Problem: Florida must not only find enough teachers and principals (quantity), but must ensure we have the great teachers and principals that our students need to succeed academically (quality).

High-quality teaching is the most important factor in improving student learning. Although money is not everything, better pay may be part of the solution to attract more qualified teachers. The "public school system currently offers virtually no incentives to reward excellence, and a system that does not reward excellence is unlikely to inspire it," said former IBM chief Lois V. Gerstner. Teachers are responsible for preparing all other members of society with the skills to succeed in life, and teachers should thus be held to the highest standards. However, many principals and teachers lack proper training. If schools are to be transformed into results-producing

If excellence is not rewarded, it is not inspired.

organizations, educators must be adequately paid and properly trained.

> **Solution: Florida must greatly enhance its teacher and principal training reforms in order to achieve real success in student academic outcomes.**

A recurring theme heard in idearaisers from Pensacola to Key West is the need for Florida to recruit and retain the best and brightest education professionals. A common proposal is to <u>pay teachers and principals based on performance and merit.</u> Such a system would reward principals for well-run schools and teachers for their abilities and efforts in the classroom. Merit determinations could be based in part on administrative evaluations, parental surveys, and student test scores. Performance/merit pay would be an incentive for Florida teachers and principals to focus on what really matters: student performance. In the 2006 session, the Legislature created the STAR (Special Teachers Are Rewarded) Plan and allocated $147 million for teacher performance/merit pay for teachers and school-based administrators. In the words of the Koret Task Force Report, "STAR allocates funds to schools based on the gains in student performance that are accomplished, giving each school a fiscal incentive to boost student performance. In this regard, Florida is leading the nation. Although other states are moving in this direction, none matches Florida in terms of magnitude, breadth, and focus." The STAR Plan should be made permanent, but with increased funding. Corporate sponsors could also fund teacher merit pay for those teaching in specified areas. Additional options include a constitutional amendment enabling the Legislature to set minimum and average teacher salaries or to enact a comprehensive teacher pay scale; or, since good principals recognize their best teachers, letting principals manage pay plans within their schools.

IDEA
16

Higig-quality teachers require continuous training. Florida provides school districts with $18 million annually for professional development for teachers, but many of these classes do not meet practical needs. For example, such courses often concentrate on "diversity" and "tolerance" instead of the new science of reading pedagogy. We will <u>require the statewide development and delivery of improved professional development courses for teachers and principals that emphasize our new curricular standards and have measurable outcomes based on both student assessment and teacher statewide competency tests.</u> These courses can be conducted online, through virtual means, or by satellite/cable in the classroom. Our new curriculum framework will define our goals for the instruction that our principals will lead, our teachers will teach, and our students will know.

IDEA

17

These training courses will establish statewide standardized professional development requirements for education professionals and will be accountable for tracking and posting participants' outcomes. Procuring top-notch training for teachers and administrators is vital to providing quality education for Florida's children, and our students would benefit from a program that properly equips teachers and demands the best from potential principals. School districts will be encouraged to develop flexible schedules that allow for professional training and staff development during the regular school work week.

As the executive in charge of a school's daily operations, a principal is responsible for the education of hundreds, sometimes thousands, of students. Schools with a capable executive have a much better chance to succeed than schools lacking an effective leader. Too often these positions have a high turnover rate. Many principals lack proper training, forcing them to learn on the job. A growing number of states, recognizing that pre-service education programs are failing to equip principals with the necessary skills, are turning to other training methodologies, such as public-private partnerships or contracting with private foundations. Furthermore, administrators can improve their leadership skills by soliciting the advice of retired principals or CEOs. Florida has many great CEOs and retired business leaders who would love to help. Chris Wittle, CEO of Edison Schools, asks, "Shouldn't we have 'principal colleges' that look more like medical schools, that are as rigorous as law schools, and that are as practical as flight school?" Florida will encourage collaboration among universities, businesses, education colleges, and specialty public-private partnerships to provide excellent principal preparation programs.

IDEA 18

If schools are to be transformed into results-producing organizations, teachers must be properly trained in an actual classroom. Since teachers are the primary non-familial adults who influence our children, they must be competent and properly prepared. Teachers need a high degree of computer literacy and technological proficiency to produce students ready for the twenty-first century.

Teachers who cannot demonstrate their competence should not be allowed to teach. To ensure the currency of teachers' skills, Florida will create statewide competency tests based on our new curricular standards for both new and veteran teachers at each grade level and subject area. Teachers will be required to pass these tests to begin teaching or to continue to teach, and to become eligible for merit pay increases. With adequate motivation and preparation for entering the education field and regular testing to ensure teachers' skills remain current, the entire education system will be transformed. Florida will be one step closer to providing a quality education for every student.

IDEA 19

Florida will need to recruit thousands of new teachers over the next decade. The characteristics of teachers that matter most are their cognitive abilities and their substantive knowledge. Florida can dramatically expand the supply of teachers *and* increase their quality if it takes the right kind of innovative actions.

In addition to streamlining traditional teacher preparation programs (see Idea 31), Florida should reform its alternative certification procedures in order to drastically reduce barriers to entry and to simplify the process for capable people to enter the teaching force. Virtually all after-hours requirements—particularly those involving the "Educator Accomplished Practices"—should be jettisoned, as should the Professional Education Test. Any person who holds a bachelor's degree and demonstrates substantive competence by having the relevant college degree in a specified area, or by passing a rigorous test, should be *fully certified* to teach in Florida's schools after passing a background check. For career and technical teachers, substantive competence can be demonstrated by mastery in a skill, such as a master plumber or auto mechanic, in place of a bachelor's degree. The districts should provide their teachers with mentoring and on-the-job training to enhance their performance, and districts should remove new teachers who do not perform adequately after a sufficient period of time, as demonstrated by their results on the new statewide competency tests, the performance of their students, and other measures.

To complement a system that reduces barriers to entry, actively seeks out career-changers, and gives the districts the largest possible pool of candidates to choose from, the state should increase the probationary period for teachers from three (the current norm) to five years, thus allowing the districts a reasonable length of time to observe the performance of new teachers and make informed decisions about whom to keep.

We will also <u>protect our teachers by insulating them from liability.</u> Florida teachers should not have to worry about accusations and lawsuits, and they deserve the full protection of the state. We need to provide peace of mind to our teachers and give them full coverage and protection. The state will effectively communicate this program and its benefits to all Florida teachers.

Finally, Florida needs to ensure school funding is spent effectively to meet the needs of each school. Therefore, Florida will <u>consider piloting student-based funding programs,</u> closely monitoring these experiments both to determine whether schools with greater control of funds become more productive and to identify spending patterns that are conducive to our goals. In this way, we will be able to analyze the true cost-effectiveness of different schools, principals, teachers, instructional materials, and programs. Greater decision-making authority at the school level within a strong accountability system that carefully measures results, demands strong student outcomes, closes unproductive schools, eliminates ineffective principals and teachers, and provides multiple options for parents and students will lead to innovative, effective, world-class schools.

Successful implementation of this greater flexibility will require:

1. Moving budget authority from the district to the school without allowing districts to reduce services or increase their costs.

2. True cost accounting/zero-based budgeting.

3. Enhancing principals' decision-making authority over personnel.

4. Better principal training and professional development.

5. Rewarding well-performing principals with monetary or decision-making awards.

6. Overcoming any constitutional issues/legal precedent over authority of elected superintendents.

7. Increased funding and implementation of programs that pair business executives with principals for mentoring in good business practices when such programs positively impact student learning and retention of effective teachers.

8. Allowing well-performing principals to set the pay level of teachers in their schools.

9. Training principals in the importance of every Florida graduate leaving school industry-certified and ready to succeed in the world of work, postsecondary education, or both.

> "Education must provide the opportunities for self-fulfillment; it can at best provide a rich and challenging environment for the individual to explore, in his own way." *Noam Chomsky*

Empowering Parents and Students

Problem: Florida needs to further integrate the principles of freedom, competition, and choice into the education marketplace.

Parental involvement is at the heart of education. Parents know their children best, love them most, and are in the best position to know if a school is successfully teaching their children. Consequently, parents should have the means and ability to influence their children's education. Giving parents the opportunity to choose their children's school is the most direct way for parents to influence their children's education. One size does not fit all in education any more than it does in clothing. Parents should be able to choose the education best suited for their children, and children should have the opportunity to receive the education most suited to their particular needs. At the same time, it is essential to maintain a system that provides quality education for all children.

Parents are best suited to choose the education options for their child.

The Koret Task Force Report praises Florida's school choice programs as "comprehensive yet simple," noting that Florida stands out "partly because some of its choice programs are unique, but mainly because Florida simultaneously offers multiple programs. Each program is relatively pure, in that sense of being designed around a particular, classic vision of school choice....In short, Florida offers a tapestry of school choice programs, and the success of the state's choice initiatives depends on this tapestry approach to coverage."

Vito Fossella (R-New York) introduced a bill in the House of Representatives to create a federal tax credit of $4,500 per family to offset the cost of private or parochial school tuition. In Florida a student qualifying for school choice would receive less than $3,500. Nationally, the amount provided to parents to cover some form of private education ranges between $3,000 and $4,500. Florida school districts, meanwhile, receive about $10,000 per student enrolled in a public school. That is why school choice means more money for education without raising the tax burden. Moreover, schools perform better when they are subject to competition and choice.

Thus the answer to Florida's education woes is not more spending but smarter spending. Success is not defined by per student spending or classroom size but by learning outcomes.

Solution: Preserve Florida's tapestry of school choice programs, and give Florida's parents and students additional education choice options.

At a series of idearaisers, attendees recognized the necessity of giving parents school choice, offering expanded opportunities for students, and retaining graduates in critical professions. They understood that giving parents school choice means more money for public schools, better matches between children and the schools they attend, and better public schools. At the end of the day, the ultimate beneficiaries of school choice are the children.

One of the cornerstones of our A+ Plan's school accountability system is to let students in failing schools transfer to a higher performing public school or a private school. This was Florida's Opportunity Scholarship Program, which was unfortunately struck down by the Florida Supreme Court. In the words of the Koret Task Force Report, "The Opportunity Scholarship Program enhanced the performance of some of the worst schools in the state, a record of accomplishment....Although the program in its current form has been ruled unconstitutional, the Florida Legislature should continue to explore ways of extending it. If the program is restored, school eligibility for participation in the program should be less stringent so that more schools are challenged by the OSP option."

We know competition drives performance. A Manhattan Institute study concluded that the availability of school vouchers has driven improvement in Florida's failing schools; researchers in two other studies reached the same conclusion. In effect, the court has removed one of the most effective tools for improving the quality of Florida's public schools. Choice opponents hailed the decision as a victory for education.

Our first priority, however, should be parents and students and how to empower them. We must focus on what is best for students, not systems.

The heated rhetoric surrounding school choice and other education reform issues makes it hard for parents to know what is going on, and makes it far too easy to forget we are talking about our children's futures. Our schools must help each child achieve his or her potential. If our schools are not meeting the challenge, parents should have other options. Florida must <u>continue to add options for student and parent choice in education.</u> School choice options will protect quality education offered at public schools and benefit children in all schools.

IDEA 24

Florida will consider offering parents the following types of education options:

1. Scholarships to the school of their choice for foster children.

2. Scholarships to the school of their choice for adopted children.

3. Scholarships to the school of their choice for limited English proficient students or English language learners.

4. Scholarships to the school of their choice for children at risk of dropping out of school.

5. A pilot program whereby individual school districts can "choose" to make their entire school district an open full school choice district in exchange for state rewards.

6. An increased statewide cap (from the current $88 million) on corporate tax credit scholarships, which provide school choice options for economically disadvantaged families. The income

eligibility for this program should also be increased to enable more students to participate.

7. Increased sources that fund the corporate tax credit scholarship program. This would increase the number of businesses in the program and provide companies with greater flexibility to choose credits that impact their tax liability. Floridians should also be allowed to donate funds for school choice options for economically disadvantaged families when they annually register their cars, just as they can make other types of donations at that time. Consider a specialty license tag for school choice options for economically disadvantaged families.

Another education option for parents will be an increase in virtual schooling. Florida has some very successful virtual school programs. The Florida Virtual School allows all Florida students (public, private, and home-schooled) in grades 7–12 to take individual courses online. There are also two K–8 virtual schools whereby current public school students or kindergarten and first grade students can take their entire elementary or middle school coursework online. Parents love the flexibility of these programs. Florida will remove the limits on the number of students who can participate in the K–8 virtual school programs and the eligibility requirement that students must have been in the public school system the prior school year. This will enable the full participation of private or home-schooled students, as is the case with the Florida Virtual School.

More virtual schooling options will also be created. Florida has thousands of state-certified teachers who are no longer teaching in Florida public schools. If we can create more virtual environments whereby these certified teachers could teach remotely from home, we could tap into this vast pool of educators and provide greater choice for parents.

IDEA
26

Finally, Florida will <u>identify professions in high demand that are currently experiencing shortages</u> (for example, mathematicians, scientists, nurses, engineers, and teachers) and provide incentives for students to remain in Florida and enter these professions. Possible incentives include removing unnecessary prerequisites and reducing tuition and/or offering scholarships to students who pursue majors in these fields and who agree to work in Florida for a set number of years following graduation. Citizens who become military personnel and complete their contracts should also be eligible for these scholarships based solely on their most recent SAT or ACT scores. When these students graduate and enter the workforce, they could also be given signing bonuses.

> *"The truth is that the want of common education with us is not from our poverty, but from the want of an orderly system. More money is now paid for the education of a part than would be paid for that of the whole if systematically arranged."* Thomas Jefferson

School System Reforms

Problem: We need to incorporate more efficiency, streamlining, and competition into the school system to make it responsive to students and parents.

There are many hardworking teachers, principals, and superintendents in Florida. However, sometimes these individuals work against a structure or traditions that do not support their efforts. The system must be constantly evaluated to provide an effective, efficient, safe, and high quality education system.

Moreover, our current spending on the school system as a whole could be more effective. Florida spends billions of dollars annually on facilities, transportation, and food services for its public school system. If Florida introduced competition, the resulting savings could be used to fund items such as teacher salaries, school materials, and school programs.

Florida must focus on goals not system tradition in the education of our children.

At an idearaiser on July 17, 2006, participants from across the state reiterated an argument frequently made at other idearaisers: there is a critical need for higher standards in school accountability, from the budget process to fostering relationships with private partners to aid in school construction.

Solution: Reevaluate and improve the structure, funding, and management of Florida's school system.

IDEA 27

Florida will <u>provide voters with the option of dividing large school districts into smaller districts.</u> Florida has some of the nation's largest school districts and the highest number of large districts of any state in the nation. Some of our school districts are so large they suffer from diseconomies of scale. Even though the creation of smaller school districts would increase administrative costs due to new superintendents and transportation systems, many of these costs are less than the diseconomies of scale found in large districts that have multiple assistant district administrators. Smaller districts would create more equity among schools and, most importantly, would make the district administration more accessible to the parents and students, thus enhancing parental involvement. Creation of smaller school districts would have to be implemented by a constitutional amendment.

IDEA 28

To ensure school funds are properly spent, Florida will <u>create and fund an Inspector General or other watchdog to track incidents of fraud, waste, and abuse that occur each year in Florida public schools.</u> This watchdog will report in a simple and easy to understand format, by county, the following incidents: reported teacher abuse, sex offenses, and molestation; reported fraud in construction and overpayments for contracts;

reported cases of school staff or teachers charged with DUI, theft, and FCAT cheating; and reported school board, superintendent, or administrative impropriety.

To ensure greater fiscal accountability, Florida will <u>require all schools that accept state funds, including community colleges and universities, to send parents annual notices delineating school content, performance, and spending.</u> The notices should clearly explain the expenditures made for each student, including monies spent on state-of-the-art classrooms and technology. Additionally, the notices should clearly relate a school's effectiveness in terms of student achievement outcomes and graduation rates, so that citizens will be able to see the return on investment.

To monitor the success of our education system, we will <u>charge the Department of Education with annually evaluating the performance of the graduates of the state-approved teacher preparation programs.</u> There are currently ten public universities and eighteen private institutions that have state approval for traditional teacher preparation programs. We now have data to analyze the effectiveness of these programs' graduates, based upon the learning gains of their students. The public reporting of these data will enable school districts to recruit from the better-performing schools, thus forcing the other programs to improve and update their instruction. Continued approval of a teacher preparation program by the State Board will be made depend on the level of success achieved by the program's graduates. In addition to streamlining alternative teacher certification processes (see Idea 20), we will <u>streamline the traditional state-approved teacher preparation programs offered by colleges of education by revising mandatory, uniform core curricula and pre-service field experience requirements.</u> New standards will require three years of instruction for the uniform core curricula requirements and one year paid student teaching to meet the pre-service field requirement.

IDEA
32

Florida will also <u>provide incentives to create innovative public-private partnerships that will expand after-school programs</u> for student sports, physical education, arts, music, mentoring, and educational improvement. Regional Athletic Clubs, Boys' and Girls' Clubs, 4H Clubs, YMCAs, and others might be eager to participate. These programs should have strong account-ability measures for outcomes to justify their funding. Parents would love to have the opportunity for their children to be in these well-supervised and educationally beneficial programs rather than having "latch-key kids" loitering at the malls or at home watching television at home.

In addition to providing Florida's children with supervised, instructional after-school programs, Florida needs to create more classrooms. A constantly growing population and limited amounts of space and funds has created a classroom shortage. Florida needs new schools, and it needs them quickly. This shortage, combined with the constitutional class size amendment that will soon take full effect, means that Florida is on the verge of a crisis in terms of its available education space.

IDEA
33

Florida should <u>pursue public-private partnerships to provide classroom construction, leasing, main-tenance, and school services.</u> Public-private part-nerships are contractual agreements between the government (local or state) and a private company that combine the resources of both to provide services to the public. The private partner then contributes capital in return for the government's promise to repay the initial cost over a period of time. These partnerships benefit all involved—most importantly the taxpayers—and their use should be welcomed and increased in Florida.

Several states utilize public-private partnerships, most often for new school construction. Ronald D. Utt, Ph.D., a Fellow at the Heritage Foundation and author of several articles on such partnerships, estimates the average tax savings at 15 percent. These savings come from a combination of tax-exempt borrowing privileges and streamlined construction regulations. The school system is rewarded with shorter construction times and minimal up-front capital investment. Some schools using this partnership agreement have been built in nine months, as opposed to the average of five years.

Public-private partnerships are beneficial tools, allowing governments to provide better public services at a lower cost, while maintaining account-ability. We have already seen their success in Florida. In 1999, Ryder System, Inc. built a school across from its headquarters in Miami-Dade County for its employees and local residents. At the time Ryder built the school, the average school construction project took between three and five years from design to completion. Ryder built its school, adhering to all applicable standards and school district codes, in just nine months. A similar project was recently completed in Sumter County by the Villages, a 12,000 acre development in central Florida. The Villages built an elementary, middle, and high school in just over one year, complying with all standards and requirements of Sumter County.

Public-private partnering has already proven effective and its success will surely continue. We will establish a high-level task force—independent of special interest—to study optimal methods of public-private partnering.

To facilitate the building of new schools, Florida will extend its sales tax exemption for school construction materials to pre-approved contractors and subcontractors on a project-by-project basis. Contractors will have to go through a competitive bidding process to become pre-approved. Allowing contractors to purchase their construction materials directly and receive the school construction materials exemption from the sales tax will ensure sales tax dollars are not spent on school buildings. Private sector efficiency can build schools in a fraction of the time while still ensuring safety and quality. Putting companies that specialize in construction in charge of building schools, rather than school boards that lack the expertise and technical acumen of general contractors, makes sense.

Public-private partnerships could also be extended to the provision of other school services. Privatizing school services such as transportation in numerous states, including Illinois and Alabama, resulted in substantial financial savings and improved service quality. A study by Ball State University estimates public ownership of school bus services costs a school district up to 12 percent more than the price to contract with a private vendor. Moreover, a 1998 study by Florida's Office of Program Policy Analysis and Government Accountability found that privatized school transportation could save Florida over $13 million annually. Another area to examine for public-private partnerships is school provision of cafeteria food. In sum, public-private partnerships will enable schools to free up money for other educational uses.

Every year millions of classroom dollars are denied to students from the refusal to explore privatization options.

CHAPTER

II

Restoring Accountability and Delivering Results

IDEA

34

Florida Government Accountability Act

Problem: Agencies and their advisory committees lack program reviews and assessment mechanisms.

Agencies and their advisory committees should be assessed periodically to determine their efficiency. Floridians want a system to ensure each taxpayer dollar is spent to address current priorities. They want a system that eliminates spending on unnecessary or obsolete programs by forcing a program's proponents to justify, on a regular basis, the need for the program and its benefits.

Solution: Create and empower the Legislative Sunset Advisory Committee.

The 2006 Legislature created the Florida Government Accountability Act, which authorized the creation of a Legislative Sunset Advisory Committee. Florida should create and empower this committee, whose membership will include both senators

IDEA

34

and representatives, in order to increase the effectiveness of the review process established by the Act.

The committee is modeled after the Texas Sunset Review Commission, which was established to review all of the state's agencies, programs, and boards. Ultimately, the Texas Commission abolished forty-seven agencies, programs, or boards, saving $736.9 million in taxpayer dollars. Like the Texas Commission, the Legislative Sunset Advisory Committee will systematically review *all* the duties, operations, and programs of state agencies and their advisory committees. The committee should also determine whether certain public/private entities have upheld their promises to increase job opportunities, tourism, and state income. The scheduled sunset reviews allow all stakeholders, the Legislature, the executive branch, and any interested citizens to evaluate programs' relevancy, necessity, effectiveness, and possible improvements in a coordinated manner. Many agencies and programs may continue unaltered after the review; however, having been subjected to a critical review these programs will hold a greater accountability than any non-reviewed program.

The Texas Commission saved $736.9 million in taxpayer dollars.

Beginning in 2008, the reviews will be staggered by agency or advisory committee. This provides interested parties and stakeholders with advance notice in order to prepare for the review, allows the Legislature time to evaluate a committee's work, and allows the Committee to conduct its own in-depth review. Overall, requiring an automatic sunset of all newly created advisory committees, boards, and commissions would greatly promote the mission of the Florida Government Accountability Act.

Procedures for mandatory sunset reviews will provide necessary incentives to agencies, stakeholders, and the Legislature to conduct reviews diligently while also providing accountability to Florida's citizens. The committee will send an unequivocal message that Florida is serious about streamlining government and acting as fiscally responsible stewards of taxpayer dollars.

"There is not a more important or fundamental principle in Legislation... that our appropriations should go hand in hand with our promises." James Madison

Policy Choices Should Drive Budget Choices

Problem: A bifurcated process insulates budget decisions from policy considerations.

Policy and budgetary decisions are inextricably linked. Unfortunately, government spending decisions too often drive policy instead of the other way around. In Florida, the organizational structure of the Legislature is a major contributing factor to this problem.

The Florida House of Representatives is comprised of twenty-eight substantive standing committees under nine councils and seven fiscal committees under one fiscal council. Generally, bills are first referred and heard in one or several substantive committees for policy development and then, if a bill has a fiscal impact, it is referred to a fiscal committee or the fiscal council for budgetary considerations. Next, the bill goes back to a substantive council, then to the House floor for a vote by the members.

The process of developing policy and budget in separate committees is problematic. The substantive committees and fiscal committees each have independent staffs with different skills. Substantive staff has detailed knowledge in their particular policy area, which they use to assist members in crafting bill language appropriate to accomplish the members' policy objectives. Fiscal staff has more generalized knowledge of policy but focus more on budgetary aspects of the proposed legislation. The result of this bifurcated process is that good policy is often modified or killed in the fiscal committee in order to balance the state budget.

Past efforts to correct this situation have been inadequate. Substantive and fiscal committees often share the same group of members. The bill analysis presented to substantive committee includes a section on fiscal impact, so substantive committee usually has some awareness of the cost of proposed legislation. But substantive committees often do not know whether funds are available for the proposed legislation. This decision is often not made until later in the session after the Speaker has assessed priorities, including substantive and budgetary priorities, the need for member projects, and the revenues available based on the most recent revenue estimating conference.

Another factor contributing to this problem is the reluctance of members to vote against a bill in its first committee of reference. Thus, a practice has evolved to extend a courtesy to a bill sponsor in a substantive committee to vote the bill out of committee and "fix it at the next stop," which is usually an appropriations committee or the floor. Thus, a practice has evolved to direct the fiscal committee to fix these flaws or let the bill die in committee. This "blunt instrument" approach to dealing with bills in the fiscal committee has frustrated many bill sponsors. A better process is needed.

Solution: Remove the procedural and structural impediments to achieving a policy-driven budget.

The solution is for the House to <u>combine fiscal and</u> <u>substantive committees into a single committee</u> <u>that will develop and fund the most appropriate</u> <u>policy issues for Florida.</u> Additionally, the budget should be restructured into a more user-friendly document that provides agencies with greater flexibility to accomplish the desired policy objectives. Finally, the format of the budget should be revised to provide agencies with greater flexibility to more efficiently accomplish the desired policy objectives. Fiscal and substantive staff will work together in the committee suite instead of being segregated, and committee members and the chairman will simultaneously decide policy and budgetary issues. This will require several process adjustments. Policy and budget considerations must be aligned to stay within available resources. In addition, bills with policy flaws must be corrected and ready for Floor action before being voted out of committee.

The budget's format, which is incomprehensible to the public and even to most legislators, needs revision. The format of Florida's General Appropriations Act displays budget in traditional categories, indicating by agency, program area, service, and fund the amount appropriated for items such as salaries, expenses, contractual services, and fixed capital outlays. This type of display allows for a view of the budget in total, but lacks information on changes that occurred between budgets and why these changes were made. For example, one may compare annual budgets and discover that contractual services increased in a particular program from one year to the next, but no explanation for the funding hike will be found unless it is spelled out in proviso.

Embedded in the budgetary system, however, are details showing how general appropriations acts are developed. Given the example of an increase in a program's contractual services, the detail in the budget system will show the reason for the increase (e.g., the state was purchasing an increased amount of services). However, this detail is not included in the printed version of the General Appropriations Act.

IDEA 36

Florida will <u>design an e-budget website that will display a detailed, issue-level budget and allow the public to comment on the budget.</u> This budget will be restructured from an input-based methodology appropriating money for employees, salaries, travel, furniture, and contracts, to a results-based approach.

The new e-budget will allow residents to view the funding details of the budget's service or program areas by category. Viewers will see the budget at various levels of complexity: departmental, program, service, and issue. The budget will be far more transparent and understandable.

Another problem is the Legislature's approach to appropriating funds. Funds are appropriated based on program inputs such as number of employees managing the program, their travel budget, how much they can spend on contracts with vendors, advertising, and so on. This approach hinders the program managers from designing and implementing the most cost-effective methods of management. For example, instead of having state employees deliver food service for a correctional institution, it may be more cost-effective to award this service to a private vendor. In fact, the Bush administration saved almost $61 million by outsourcing prison food services. Thus, program managers would be able to allocate resources in the most appropriate fashion to accomplish the most cost-effective program outcomes.

Tax dollars should be used to purchase results not wasted funding inputs without regard to performance.

> *"If liberty and equality, as is thought by some, are chiefly to be found in democracy, they will be best attained when all persons alike share in the government to the utmost."* Aristotle

Securing Florida's Place on the National Stage

Problem: Florida lacks real influence in national primaries.

Given the opportunity and importance of the early primary contests, at least one early state primary should reflect the country's diversity. None of the states with earlier primaries that Florida's can match our
Floridians should have a more influential role in choosing national candidates.
diversity in population (both ethnic and socio-economic), varied landscape of productive farmland, growing suburbs, vibrant cities, and range of ecosystems. The impact of this diversity would manifest itself on election day.

With a voter turnout rate of 64 percent, Florida allows candidates to be judged by a diverse population of over 7 million people. New Hampshire, with fewer than 500,000 voters in its primary, and Iowa, with fewer than 200,000 participants, simply cannot match the range of issues found in Florida, with its large, diverse population that reflects America's overall demographics. Given Florida's significant impact on general elections, its citizens should have an active, influential voice in the process of choosing national candidates.

Solution: Force candidates to appeal to Florida's population prior to obtaining their parties nomination.

C urrently, a small, non-diverse group of citizens (the voters of Iowa and New Hampshire) have a disproportionate impact on the nomination of presidential candidates. While these states provide the benefit of beginning the presidential election in small communities that can be easily traversed and thoroughly campaigned, a large and diverse state should follow them. Without such a bellwether state on the heels of Iowa and New Hampshire, many groups of Americans will be denied a voice in selecting the most qualified candidate. The only way to change the status quo is to force candidates to be tested by more diverse populations and to address a wider range of issues. Holding Florida's primary earlier would apply that force.

The selection of national candidates should not be left to a small group of party elites.

M oving Florida's presidential primary to a time that would highlight Florida's concerns and issues would ensure our national influence in choosing a presidential candidate. Florida's population and the issues Floridians face closely mirror those of America. Consequently, an ability to appeal to Florida is an ability to appeal to America at large. Candidates would be required to become familiar with the challenges Floridians face, address issues we believe are important, and inform Floridians about their views on those issues. When those candidates are subsequently nominated, there is a greater

**IDEA
37**

chance they will be able to address the issues facing Florida and, therefore, America.

Holding Florida's primaries earlier in the year is accompanied by a host of economic benefits. The media, candidates, and special interest groups will spend millions of dollars for political advertising and spending for food, lodging, and transportation. The economic benefits to New Hampshire alone are estimated at over $100 million dollars. Florida is more than six times larger than New Hampshire.

IDEA

38

> *"The government, which was designed for the people, has got into the hands of the bosses and their employers, the special interests."* Woodrow Wilson

Protecting the Citizen Initiative Process from Special Interests

Problem: Special interests misuse the citizen initiative process.

Florida's Constitution is commonly viewed as the easiest in the United States to amend. Article XI of the Florida Constitution allows for voters to approve state constitutional amendments proposed via the following methods: proposal by joint resolution passed by a three-fifths vote of each house of the Legislature; proposal by a constitutional convention; proposal by the Constitution Revision Commission; proposal by the Taxation and Budget Reform Commission; or proposal by citizen initiative petition.

Florida adopted the citizen initiative process in 1968. The process, originally created to empower citizens to amend their constitution, has morphed into an expensive undertaking dominated by special interest groups

Big money special interest groups should not be given ownership of our Constitution.

that pay professional signature gatherers to collect petition signatures. Florida law currently permits signature gatherers to be paid by the number of signatures collected. In fact, one group boasts it can collect 1 million signatures within seventy days. That figure is well above the 611,009 signatures required for ballot certification in 2006.

Some of the recent amendments to Florida's Constitution have created huge financial commitments for our taxpayers. Legislative analysts estimate that one particular amendment will cost $400 to $500 million a year for the next five years, while another will cost Florida's taxpayers an estimated $25 billion through the 2010–2011 fiscal year. In 2005, a joint resolution was introduced in the Legislature requiring any proposed amendment, regardless of its source, that imposes a certain cost on state or local government to pass by at least a two-thirds vote. Such a proposal deserves renewed consideration.

Many argue that Florida's Constitution should set forth the fundamental and organic laws of the state instead of introducing new state policies or programs. Examples of citizen initiatives adopted during the 2004 general election include limits on attorneys' fees in medical malpractice cases, authorization of the use of slot machines in two south Florida counties, and an increase in the minimum wage. These provisions do not belong in our Constitution. The purposes of these amendments could have been accomplished by legislative action without a constitutional amendment, or with an amendment that merely authorized rather than directly implemented the underlying policy.

Grass roots citizens' groups are no longer getting their issues on the ballot—it is the well-financed, sophisticated special interest groups that are successfully amending Florida's Constitution. During the 2006 legislative session, a bill was sponsored to establish a number of safeguards for the citizen initiative process, including closer regulation of the petition verification process, requiring the provision of additional information to voters who sign an initiative petition, and regulating circulators, in particular *paid* circulators, by requiring greater disclosure. The bill died on the House calendar on the last day of session.

Solution: Reduce or eliminate the influence of special interests in the citizen initiative process.

Florida will enact legislation to reduce the growth of the paid petition business and the influence of moneyed special interests in the citizen initiative process. Legislation should require paid circulators to wear a badge identifying themselves as paid circulators; prohibit a petition sponsor from compensating any paid petition circulators if the sponsor has filed an oath of undue burden; prohibit compensation of petition circulators on a "per signature" basis; and create a process for revoking one's own signature on a petition form. These changes would help return the citizen initiative process to its original intention when adopted in 1968.

IDEA 38

In addition, Florida should consider heightened scrutiny of proposals that carry significant costs to Florida's taxpayers and determine how appropriate some proposals may be for placement in Florida's Constitution.

CHAPTER

III

Safe Homes, Safe Streets, Safe Communities

> *"Public safety is the single most
> important job of government."*
> Mitt Romney

Life Without Exception for Sexual Predators

Problem: Insufficient prison sentences are given to convicted sexual predators, and there is inadequate DNA collection for sexually deviant misdemeanors.

With increased media coverage, Floridians have become aware of the dangers sexual offenders present to our communities. A study released in 2000 indicates juveniles under eighteen years old account for 67 percent of all reported sexual assault victims (children under age twelve account for 34 percent, and children under six account for 14 percent). The highly publicized, tragic murders of Jessica Lunsford and Carlee Brucia highlighted the need for increased penalties and oversight of convicted sexual predators. Idearaiser participants repeatedly insisted that we better protect the most vulnerable members of our society. Although Florida had passed the Jessica Lunsford Act ("Jessica's law"), participants felt the Legislature needed to do more to keep our children safe from sexual predators.

Convicted sexual criminals consistently display higher recidivism rates than those convicted of other crimes. A 2003 Department of Justice study found that sex offenders' recidivism rates were four times higher than those of non–sex offenders.

Florida law enforcement officials currently collect DNA samples from people convicted of certain felony offenses. Florida has not expanded the database to include samples from all convicted felons. However, many times those convicted of felonies have prior misdemeanor convictions that signal the likelihood that they will commit more serious crimes. This was vividly illustrated in a New York case in which a man with prior misdemeanor convictions was arrested for a felony. This allowed for DNA collection linking him with two murders and a rape that might have been prevented had DNA tests been allowed for the man's prior misdemeanors. This incident spurred New York to propose DNA testing for all misdemeanors, a process in place in twenty-eight states. Currently, Florida law does not authorize the collection of DNA samples from those convicted of misdemeanor offenses.

Solution: Toughen prison sentences to keep Florida's children safe from sexual predators, and expand DNA collection to include all felony offenses and sexually deviant misdemeanors.

We must deal with sexual predators swiftly and harshly. Mandatory minimum sentences are an effective way to keep sexual predators off the street. While Jessica's law dictates mandatory minimum sentences for those convicted of sexual crimes against children under the age of twelve, mandatory minimum sentences should be applied to other sexual offenses as well.

Currently, the "dangerous sexual felony offender" act requires a minimum twenty-five-year sentence and authorizes life in prison for a second conviction of a specified felony sexual offense.

Florida should <u>expand the dangerous sexual felony offender law</u> so that all second-time sex offenders are subject to a minimum twenty-year sentence. The act will also provide a mandatory life sentence for all third-time offenders. It will also allow misdemeanor sex offenses to be enhanced to felonies and apply the enhanced penalties to those crimes.

IDEA 39

We should also <u>expand DNA collection by 2012 to include all those convicted of felony offenses and those who have exhibited a propensity for sexually deviant behavior through commission of specified misdemeanor offenses.</u> DNA collection is the modern equivalent of fingerprinting and is the most effective way to match crime scene evidence with a known criminal. Expanding DNA collection to include all felony offenses and specified sexually related misdemeanors would not expand the scope of use for DNA evidence. It would only increase the amount of data collected. This expansion would require funding for the collection, testing, and maintenance of the collected DNA samples.

IDEA 40

Florida should <u>enact laws to deny registered sex offenders and stalkers access to popular Internet networking sites mostly used by underage children and install tracking equipment on their computers to monitor their use.</u>

IDEA 41

Florida Anti-Pornography Plan

Problem: The sex trade victimizes women, harms children, and destroys neighborhoods.

Our state is confronted with the problem of pornography. The amount of available pornography is growing every year, as is the number of people addicted to it. A 2000 survey by MSNBC found that over 60 percent of website visits were to pornographic sites, with over 80 percent of the visitors to such sites jeopardizing their jobs and relationships because of their commitment to the sites.

Websites not only show pornographic material; some also serve as a clearinghouse for prostitution, setting up perverse sexual activities, and adulterous affairs. These websites also affect children. An average child in Florida will be exposed to Internet pornography by the time he or she reaches age eleven. Thousands of these sites purvey child porn and allow sex offenders to solicit our children.

Women working in the pornography industry are frequently addicted to illegal drugs, suffer routine arrests, and are frequent victims of violent crimes such as rape.

The problem is not limited to the Internet. Strip clubs house a multitude of criminal activities. In one recent case in Miami, the owners of one club stole thousands in state tax revenue, encouraged numerous acts of prostitution, and provided the venue for numerous felonious activities. Many women compelled to work in strip clubs are subjected to abuse and pressured to commit illegal sex acts. Many are even denied the benefits of real employment; strip club dancers are often forced to pay fees or operate as independent contractors, and are denied workers' compensation and leave time.

The Supreme Court has ruled that outright prohibition of nude dancing or photography is unconstitutional. However, the court never found that all forms of pornography must be allowed, nor has it prohibited the regulation of strip clubs that sell alcohol. Florida must adopt regulations to halt the illegal activities occurring at strip clubs and on pornographic websites, and develop a plan to attack the adverse effects these activities create for our state.

Solution: Eliminate anonymity and increase the costs to those arrested for and/or convicted of running a business that promotes sex crimes.

Florida should increase the risk and penalties for those who are engaged in the business of promoting sex crimes. Currently, Florida statutes define the solicitation of a person under the age of

IDEA
42

eighteen for a commercial sex act as a second-degree felony. A person who forces another to engage in prostitution or who traffics another to engage in prostitution commits a second-degree felony. Florida statutes make it a third-degree felony for anyone to derive income from prostitution. This provision outlaws pimping.

Forcing or coercing someone to become a prostitute is currently only a third-degree felony. Those acts should be enhanced to first-degree felonies. If the victim is under the age of fourteen, or if the offense results in the victim's death, the crime should be punishable by life in prison. The pimping provision should also be clarified to state that any businesses or individual who derives income, *directly or indirectly*, from prostitution or other sex offenses is subject to the penalties provided for in the statute.

To rent space or operate a structure where prostitution occurs or to procure prostitution services for another are misdemeanors for first- and second-time offenders. The statute should be amended so that people who promote or allow prostitution through their businesses, including web businesses or at their property, can be charged with a felony whether or not they derive income from the transaction. The statute should target adult entertainment establishments that act as cover for prostitution. The statute should also apply to websites that allow people to set up illegal sexual encounters whether or not the website owner profits, thus creating an incentive for operators to know who is posting on their sites and what they are doing.

These statutes should further specify that those committing any of these offenses will have their property subject to the Florida Contraband Act. Anything used, including real property and vehicles, to promote or solicit prostitution should be subject to forfeiture. Law enforcement should be empowered to close these businesses and seize all their assets. By increasing the cost of doing business, Florida can prevent these illegal operations from simply starting up again.

To successfully target those profiting from prostitution, <u>whistleblower status should be afforded to everyone who reports these crimes, even if they are involved in the act</u>. As an incentive for reporting the illegal activities, whistleblowers should also receive half the proceeds from any forfeiture actions brought in the case. This will encourage those who are being exploited to come forward and help law enforcement effectively investigate these crimes, thus assisting our women and young girls to escape prostitution.

Florida will promote this plan through a large-scale advertising campaign informing those who promote illicit sex that they are not welcome in this state. The campaign will also encourage people to come forward with information regarding these destructive, demeaning crimes.

Law enforcement should be given the investigatory tools it needs to obtain the business records of anyone promoting sex crimes in order to identify the patrons. Patrons of websites and businesses that enable illegal sexual activity should also have their names placed in a registry. This will discourage people from patronizing businesses and websites that promote criminal activity.

> "*Every American deserves to live free from the fear of violent gangs.*" *Alberto R. Gonzales*

Gang/Hate Group Elimination

Problem: Florida is witnessing growing rates of gang participation and gang-related violence.

Local law enforcement agencies have identified over 760 gangs in a statewide database managed by the Florida Department of Law Enforcement. Every city from Pensacola to the Florida Keys has been identified as having gang activity. This even includes areas not typically associated with gang activity, such as rural locations, suburban neighborhoods, and schools. The Federal Bureau of Investigation reported that juvenile gang killings increased 71 percent between 1999 and 2003. Although commonly perceived as a juvenile problem, a shift in gang membership has occurred, with adults now comprising over 60 percent of "youth gang" members.

Hate groups have also proliferated. The Southern Poverty Law Center found fifty hate groups active in Florida, second only to California. The Attorney General's Office "2004 Hate Crimes in Florida" report found that 334 hate crimes were committed in Florida, an increase of almost 22 percent from the previous year. Over three-quarters of these were violent crimes and over half involved physical assaults. Most of these groups recruit members from the prison population, where people are looking for an outlet for their antisocial tendencies.

The tragedy of September 11, 2001, has revealed that gangs are also a threat to our domestic security. The deep infiltration of gangs in our society is extremely attractive to terrorist organizations. We must listen to the warnings of Former Speaker of the U.S. House of Representatives Newt Gingrich: "Fueled by the global nature of the drug trade, gangs are increasingly international operations. With the infrastructure in place to move and distribute drugs across the border, the danger exists that they will use their network to, for the right price, traffic terrorists and weapons into the country."

Solution: Give law enforcement more resources to combat the gang threat.

Florida should <u>increase funding for additional law enforcement resources to combat gang activities.</u> Despite the formation of specialized gang task forces in some areas of the state, the problem is spreading. We need to <u>increase the numbers of specialized prosecutors and gang-related law enforcement officers, and establish training programs for them to develop better methods to combat gang and hate group activity.</u>

IDEA
44

IDEA
45

Florida should pattern its gang elimination program after the successful Gang Resistance Education And Training (G.R.E.A.T.) program. G.R.E.A.T. is a curriculum-based program aimed at teaching students skills to help them avoid gangs, violence, and drugs. There is also a law enforcement officer training component to the program. Having begun as a combined effort of the U.S. Bureau of Alcohol, Tobacco, Firearms, and Explosives and the Phoenix Police Department in 1991, G.R.E.A.T. has achieved successful results and has expanded nationwide to include the Orange County, Florida, Sheriff's Office, which assists in administering the program.

In addition to G.R.E.A.T., we need to expand successful programs that enforce truancy laws. The Miami-Dade County Police Department successfully implemented such a program, which resulted in a noticeable drop in crime rates and gang activity.

Gang investigations are harder than normal criminal investigations because gang members protect each other and intimidate witnesses. Gathering the intelligence necessary to eliminate gangs often requires "under cover" police work, a time-consuming process that involves great risk. Consequently, it cannot be done by regular, uniformed street officers. Law enforcement officers willing to undertake this dangerous work to protect Florida's citizens from gang violence and other gang-related crimes deserve the full support of the state, which must expend the resources necessary to thoroughly train and equip them.

> *"Justice delayed is justice denied."* William Gladstone

Curb Endless Appeals by Convicted Felons

Problem: Endless appeals by convicted felons postpone a sense of finality and erode public confidence in the judicial system.

At town meetings, in addresses to civic groups, and in several idearaisers, citizens advocated criminal justice system reforms, voicing legitimate concerns that the current system for resolving post-conviction matters is time-consuming and expensive. Public trust and confidence is crucial for maintaining the integrity of the judicial system.

Currently, Florida inmates have the right to a direct appeal following their conviction and the right to file motions for post-conviction relief, the majority of which allege ineffective assistance of trial counsel. The court rules that govern these issues are far more generous to inmates in Florida than in other states. This problem has devel-

Other states are able to provide constitutional due process without Florida s cumbersome process.

74

oped to the point that judges and their staff now spend a large percentage of their time reviewing a tremendous volume of post-conviction motions. Appeals from these motions consume over one-third of the more than 25,000 cases filed annually in our appellate courts. Consequently, huge commitments of judicial labor are consumed on these post-conviction matters.

Even in the simplest of criminal cases, post-conviction litigation frequently continues for a minimum of three to four years, and it is not un-usual to see post-conviction motions filed five to ten years after the defendant's conviction. In death penalty cases the post-conviction process averages 12.83 years, but in some cases it has consumed up to twenty years before a warrant is signed. With over 370 inmates on death row in Florida, delays of this nature hinder justice for the victims and er-ode public confidence in Florida's criminal justice system.

Very few inmates receive actual relief from the current cumbersome, time-consuming, and expensive pro-cess. In truth, Florida's public defenders and private attorneys effectively defend their clients, and claims to the contrary are usually without merit.

Solution: Streamline the appeals process in criminal cases.

Florida should create a new, more efficient, less expensive process for reviewing criminal cases that instills more public confidence in the criminal justice system. This could be accomplished by limiting the time convicted felons have to appeal their sentences. One option is to utilize a dual track system in which the direct appeal and post-conviction proceedings occur simul-taneously. This will reduce the time and expense of litigating these cases.

IDEA

46

CHAPTER

IV

Keep Florida Moving . . . Forward

> "America's highways, roads, bridges, are
> an indispensable part of our lives. They
> link one end of our nation to the other.
> We use them each and every day, for
> every conceivable purpose." Christopher Dodd

Improving Florida's Roadways through Private Sector Involvement

Problem: Funding is inadequate to build and maintain a transportation system that meets Florida's expanding needs.

Florida's infrastructure is experiencing incredible growing pains, and there is a mammoth backlog of vital transportation improvements. Although, based on current transportation plans and anticipated state and federal revenues, Florida will invest $117 billion between now and 2025, we face a $53 billion revenue shortfall for the Strategic Intermodal System alone. In a state with thousands of new residents pouring in each month, transportation, infrastructure, and highway congestion was a primary concern of many Floridians who submitted ideas via the 100ideas website or at idearaisers hosted by Representatives. We heard our citizens voice frustration at the precious hours of family time lost due to traffic congestion, consumers' insistence that prices would fall if products could be delivered to stores faster, and testimonials that our transportation problems have lowered citizens' overall quality of life. These problems led to the repeated expression of one idea from Pensacola to Miami: the state needs to improve our transportation system today and to prepare for the transportation needs of our children.

Solution: Government should collaborate with the private sector to fund, build, and maintain needed transportation improvements.

IDEA

47

Florida will <u>partner with private companies to build a model transportation system that will provide the highest quality of life for our citizens.</u> To do so, we must combine the best practices of the private sector with the safeguards of government to create a true partnership that will benefit all Floridians.

Florida has been partnering with the private sector for many years to improve transportation. Currently, the private sector provides services in such areas as road and bridge construction, engineering design, construction inspection, roadway maintenance, and toll collections. In addition, the private sector has partnered with the Department of Transportation via land donations, cash contributions, road and interchange construction, and related issues over the past ten years in a value exceeding $1 billion.

In Europe, Asia, Australia, and South America, the private sector has been providing comprehensive services through public-private partnerships (PPPs) to deliver transportation. These comprehensive services include design-build-finance-operate-maintain schemes, with the private sector receiving "payment" through tolls collected on a road or bridge, a direct payment from the "owner," or a combination of the two.

This model for the development of new transportation facilities is new to the United States. There are currently two functioning facilities developed under the full PPP approach: the Dulles Greenway in northern Virginia and SR-91 in California, both toll facilities. Three other extant facilities—two toll facilities and one monorail project—are hybrid PPPs funded through tax-exempt debt issued by non-profit corporations. The PPP model is rapidly spreading, with Texas, Virginia, and Oregon currently working on PPP projects to build new toll roads.

Florida has relied upon public models to develop its toll facilities, including Florida's Turnpike, expressway/bridge authorities, and the DOT. The public model has delivered a large number of toll facilities over the past forty years. Moreover, 90 percent of new roads in Florida built in the last fifteen years are toll roads/bridges. A number of toll entities have evolved into "toll systems" like Florida's Turnpike, where toll revenues from existing roads are used to leverage system improvements like widenings and also to build new expansion projects.

Florida is currently developing a PPP project for the Port of Miami Tunnel in which the private sector would design-build-finance-operate-maintain the facility and be paid, after the tunnel opens, based on the availability of the facility each year for thirty years. The payment would be funded from a combination of user fees and local and state grant funds. The key reason for utilizing a PPP for this project is to procure the technical expertise to design and build a complex tunnel. Additionally, the private sector will be assuming appropriate levels of risk to deliver the project and its future operations, maintenance, and renewals.

The PPP sector is very keen on involvement in delivering transportation improvements in Florida. The PPP model allows leveraging the private sector's innovation and ability to raise capital to help bridge Florida's capacity gap in the delivery of transportation services.

Through a successful process utilized nationally and globally, Florida will <u>lease existing toll roads to private companies.</u> Still owned by the citizens of Florida, a leased highway provides valuable income to the state to enhance other transportation projects, lowers annual maintenance costs, and allows private companies to enhance the quality of service on the highway to the residents and visitors who utilize it. These projects have proven lucrative in other regions: in 1996, Toronto received an up-front payment of $3.7 billion for a 99-year lease on the "407" commuter roadway, with the private buyer agreeing to fund numerous improvements and extensions; in 2005, Chicago agreed to a 99-year lease of the Chicago Skyway, a commuter bridge from Indiana to Chicago, for $1.83 billion; and Indiana in 2006 agreed to a 75-year lease of the Indiana Turnpike running east-west across the state for $3.85 billion.

In all three cases, the private partner provided up-front payment and agreed to operate, maintain, and repair the asset for the duration of the lease. In turn, the government allowed the private partner to retain revenues from tolls, whose rates it could raise over time based on factors such as the consumer price index, increases in gross domestic product, and related indices.

For many years, Florida has leveraged toll facilities including Florida's Turnpike, Miami-Dade County Expressways, Orlando-Orange County Expressways, and Tampa-Hillsborough County Expressways, utilizing toll revenues to widen and improve these expressways and to build new expressways. The toll rates, while not at market rates, have been increased periodically to help fund these improvements.

Florida has numerous un-leveraged toll facilities that currently have comparatively low toll rates. These include Sunshine Skyway and Alligator Alley, both part of the interstate system. Florida should examine its existing toll practices and policies and explore opportunities for privatizing roads to help fund needed transportation improvements.

Meanwhile, Florida should continue to pursue the goal of a 95 percent return on federal gasoline tax dollars from the United States Congress. Based on recent federal legislation, by 2008 Florida will receive a 92 percent rate of return on all dollars distributed.

Transportation is essential for economic activity and mobility. Commerce suffers when congestion and inadequate links between modes of transportation create costly delays. Lower-income Floridians cannot fully partake in our prosperity when a lack of transportation isolates them from jobs and economic opportunities. The Florida Chamber of Commerce Foundation analyzed transportation and economic development issues in its 1999 report, *Transportation Cornerstone Florida: Moving Florida's Economy into the 21st Century*. The report noted that "throughout its history, Florida's economy and population have been living testimony to the power of a dynamic, forward-looking transportation system. Indeed the high level of transportation service has been part of the 'fountain of youth' that

To maintain a strong economy, Florida's transportation system must meet growing demands.

has enabled Florida's economy to grow and thrive." However, the *Transportation Cornerstone* also stated the transportation system is showing "signs of falling behind the pace of economic growth and change." .

The relationship between transportation investments and Florida's economic competitiveness has received increased attention recently. An analysis presented to the 2003 Legislature demonstrated investments in highway, transit, and rail over the next five years will generate 88,000 new permanent jobs over the next twenty-five years, and each dollar invested in those projects will generate $5.50 in economic benefits. Florida should aggressively pursue public-private partnerships to address the state's transportation and economic needs.

> *"It is true that privatization has given a shot in the arm to all sorts of industries."* Barbara Castle

Privatize the Division of Drivers' Licenses

Problem: The government is inefficient at providing drivers' license services.

The Department of Highway Safety and Motor Vehicles' Division of Drivers' Licenses issues drivers' licenses and vehicle registrations and provides a variety of other services. Over time, especially with respect to drivers' licenses, customer service has not kept pace with demand or expectations. This was a common refrain among frustrated citizens at idearaisers. Previous attempts have been made to address these concerns, including use of local tax collector offices, online services, investment in infrastructure and technology, and discussions involving outsourcing or privatization. Various studies have offered conflicting recommendations. In 2006, the Legislature directed the Department to study outsourcing its driver license services and make recommendations by January 1, 2007.

Solution: Allow the private sector to operate the Division of Drivers' Licenses along with, or in lieu of, government.

S tate government must ensure its operations are not cumbersome to its citizens. The Division of Drivers' Licenses should operate with the same efficiency and quality of service expected from other businesses. Limited privatization of some duties has already been successful in North Dakota and California. In those states, driving schools and registration tasks are privatized, often to insurance companies. In Arizona and California, privatization studies have shown enormous fiscal savings. To provide the most efficient and effective services for our citizens, Florida will <u>allow private companies to operate the Division of Drivers' Licenses.</u> Privatization will reduce necessary yet burdensome constraints on the daily lives of Floridians.

IDEA

49

Florida will also <u>offer multiple-year vehicle registrations.</u> An extended validation period would minimize citizens' burden of annually renewing registrations and reduce the workload of the agency or business responsible for renewal. To encourage Floridians to utilize multiple-year registrations, citizens should receive a discount for purchasing extended registrations and additional discounts for purchasing or renewing registrations online, thereby decreasing paperwork and long lines.

IDEA

50

IDEAS

51-53

> *"Identify theft is one of the fastest-growing crimes in the nation."* Melissa Bean (D)

Protection from Identity Theft

Problem: There is an increasing number of identity theft crimes.

The increase in technology and electronic communication has left individuals exposed to the dangers of identity theft and highlighted Florida's need to increase the criminal penalties to protect its residents. In 2005, 9.3 million U.S. citizens were victims of identity fraud, while fraud costs have risen from $53.2 billion in 2003 to over $56.5 billion in 2006. Although federal legislation protects victims from the direct costs of identity theft, regaining a clean credit record and securing personal information remain priorities for the residents of Florida.

Florida's elderly are particularly at risk for fraud. Seniors often have accumulated resources such as

Governments should not partner with criminals who victimize Florida's citizens.

property, insurance and pension plans, savings, stocks and bonds, and other assets that are not always closely monitored.

The Federal Trade Commission notes identity theft targeting those over age sixty jumped from 1,800 cases in 2000 to almost 6,000 cases the following year, with most cases involving the misuse of Social Security numbers.

Victims of identity theft on average spend 175 hours trying to resolve the resulting problems. Cases take an average of twenty-three months to reach resolution. Discounting legal fees, victims can expect to spend up to $2,000 to clear their names.

Solution: Revise Florida law to better protect citizens from identity theft.

Currently for an identity theft crime to qualify as a first-degree felony, the fraud must cause at least $50,000 in damages or affect the identification information of at least twenty individuals. Florida should base the felony level of identity theft crimes on the class of victim, as well as the monetary damage incurred. In Florida, any person convicted of an identity theft crime affecting a person sixty-five years or older will face enhanced penalties.

IDEA 51

Current Florida law permits conviction for possession of another's identification information only if the state can prove intent to *use* the information. We should eliminate the "use" requirement to mirror the treatment of the possession of narcotics offenses. Florida should make any unauthorized possession of another's personal identity information a felony, regardless of use or whether monetary damage is sustained.

IDEA 52

Lastly, Florida should adopt an "opt in" policy that requires government and business to receive permission from citizens before distributing any of their personal information. Personal information should always remain

IDEA 53

private, even when collected legally. An "opt-in" requirement when government or any business requests personal identification information would help to increase consumer security by giving consumers control over who sees their information. This should apply to Internet service providers, online businesses, banks, hospitals, credit card companies, government services, and any other entity that requires personal information to conduct business. This opt-in provision would allow Floridians themselves to define the extent of protections for their personal information.

Florida cannot and will not tolerate identity theft. As technology allows for the freer flow of information, the Legislature must act decisively to protect all Floridians from the theft and misuse of their identities.

> *"'Mid pleasures and palaces though we may roam, be it ever so humble, there's no place like home."* John Howard Payne

Affordable Homeowners' Insurance for Florida

Problem: The cost of homeowners' insurance is rising.

One of the most common concerns expressed during the 100ideas process was Florida's skyrocketing homeowners' insurance rates. Florida has taken the brunt of the nation's hurricane destruction; in an eighteen-month period, Florida was struck by eight hurricanes, generating $38 billion in insured loses. Because of the frequency and devastating nature of hurricanes, hurricane insurance has risen dramatically in Florida. Consequently, insuring their homes has become a financial burden for many families, affecting the affordability of our housing stock. Homes built prior to the uniform building code cause greater risk for insurers and greater disruptions to the economic fabric of Florida's families. Over 7.3 million housing units were built in Florida prior to the new statewide building code.

Necessary homeowners' insurance has become unaffordable to many of Florida's citizens.

Solution: Assist Florida citizens to make their primary Florida residences hurricane-ready, develop more options for insurance premium discounts and deductibles, achieve premium savings through reinsurance reforms, and strengthen consumer protections and expand loan programs to help homeowners.

Safe construction is the best way to protect homes from hurricanes. Ensuring safe construction would require repairing many older homes. This would create large up-front costs ranging from a few hundred to several thousand dollars, but would result in long-term payoffs. If homes could incur only minimal to moderate damage in hurricanes as opposed to total destruction, insurance payouts would significantly decrease, thus reducing premiums, allowing more companies to enter the market, creating competition, and lowering prices. During the 2006 legislative session, the Legislature appropriated $250 million for home inspections and grants to make homes hurricane-ready. On the program's first day, over 30,000 people called to inquire if they were eligible. Florida should increase funding of home inspections and grants to upgrade homes to better withstand hurricanes by creating a recurring source of funding. Hurricane-ready homes would further drive down insurance prices and ensure greater preparedness for future storms.

**IDEA
54**

Insurance companies around the state now offer discounts and credits for hurricane mitigation. Companies provide various discounts on premiums depending upon the type of hurricane prevention. Roll-down hurricane shutters, for example, may merit a greater discount than pre-cut plywood panels. However, discounts and credits vary widely and are not presented in a manner that allows consumers to weigh the costs and benefits of hurricane mitigation expenditures. Florida should <u>ensure all insurance companies provide appropriate, easily understood credits or discounts to homeowners engaging in hurricane mitigation,</u> to encourage the average homeowner to take preventative measures.

Another issue negatively impacting homeowners throughout the state is that some insurance companies fail to insure homes based solely on their age, regardless of whether mitigation has occurred or remodeling has brought the home into compliance with more modern and stringent codes. Accordingly, the state should <u>consider adopting a uniform grading system to evaluate the hurricane strength of homes, allowing homeowners in some cases to become insured by the private market and in other cases to take full and appropriate advantage of the measures undertaken to fortify their homes.</u>

Finally regarding the physical structure of our homes, Florida's building code, designed to be uniform across jurisdictions, does not equally serve all parts of Florida. While the vast majority of Floridians benefit from the best model building codes available, variations in the code keep Panhandle citizens vulnerable to hurricanes. Our codes should protect all Floridians from the calamitous effects of wind and water in future hurricanes.

<u>Florida must ensure consistent building code practices statewide by adopting a uniform statewide building code.</u> In doing so, Florida will attract more private reinsurance to the state and decrease the chances for assessments to most property and casualty policyholders.

This statewide code should be constantly updated based on the availability of new technologies. Florida

International University is undertaking studies on how builders can construct homes to withstand a category 3 hurricane without significant damage. However, such research will be pointless if builders and municipal building departments do not respond to these findings with stronger building codes and strict adherence to them. Such actions would help save lives and reduce insurance costs.

One factor driving up the cost of homeowners' insurance is the high price that property insurers pay for reinsurance. If Florida companies could pay less for reinsurance they could provide more coverage, thereby reducing the number of people going into Citizens and inducing companies to lower prices. Currently, reinsurance is available to property insurers through the state-run Florida Hurricane Catastrophe Fund. Other possible options include the creation of a federal enterprise zone for reinsurance in Florida, and the formulation of a hurricane exchange program allowing investors to provide funds to protect insurance companies against large claims from major storms. <u>The Florida Hurricane Catastrophe Fund should allow companies to buy more reinsurance from the fund below the current retention and charge near-market rates. Alternative reinsurance mechanisms promoting competition should also be pursued.</u>

IDEA 58

There are ways to save homeowners money while providing consumers more options. To increase insurance capacity, decrease upward pressure on homeowner insurance rates, and provide an incentive for homeowners to mitigate their homes for wind damage, Florida should <u>allow insurers to offer all homeowners, with appropriate financial and guaranteed renewal incentives, policies with higher hurricane deductibles.</u>

IDEA 59

IDEA 60

Another innovative idea to encourage personal responsibility and reduce homeowners' out-of-pocket costs due to hurricane-related losses is to permit policyholders to reduce their hurricane deductible if they implement meaningful and verifiable mitigation measures.

IDEA 61

While the high price of hurricane insurance is a primary concern, we can help consumers by implementing other measures not directly related to costs. Florida homeowners deserve to be treated fairly and honestly by insurers. While market forces and competition are the best means to ensure fair treatment, some new consumer protections can also help. A comprehensive package of consumer protections should include, among other provisions, requiring a "Truth in Premium Billing" statement delineating the various components and prices of changes in premiums such as rate increases; coverage provisions and assessments; requiring insurers to offer installment payment plans on homeowner policies based upon semi-annual and quarterly scheduling; guaranteeing homeowners be provided more advance notice in cases of policy cancellations and non-renewals; and providing standards for ensuring that insurance agents' commissions are justified when homeowners experience dramatic premium increases.

IDEA 62

While protection against hurricane damage provides the best defense against financially devastating losses, some Floridians will inevitably have their homes damaged and will require quick responses from insurance companies. Other homeowners suffering more severe destruction will need financial help to rebuild. Florida lawmakers should ensure that insurance companies expedite payments for damages and consider expanding the short-term, no-interest bridge loan program that is authorized by the governor through an amendment pursuant to the declaration of a state of emergency. The loans are intended to bridge the gap between the time disaster strikes and the time repair work can be funded through insurance, long-term loans, or other means.

S tate lawmakers have been working diligently for years to address the multitude of hurricane and insurance issues facing Floridians. However, hurricanes and other natural catastrophes do not occur only in Florida. Since some assistance options can only be enacted on the federal level. the federal government must help our state and others increase the availability and affordability of property insurance. Florida should undertake a concerted, statewide, bipartisan effort to advocate for the federal government to establish a Federal Natural Catastrophe Reinsurance Fund; allow insurers to accumulate tax-deferred reserves to prepare for catastrophes and to reduce the necessity for reinsurance; and create "Hurricane Savings Accounts" permitting homeowners to set aside funds tax-free in order to purchase policies with higher deductibles. If Congress does not establish the Natural Catastrophe Reinsurance Fund, Florida should still try to spread risks through a multi-state, non-federal partnership.

F lorida must develop an innovative package of reforms to lower the cost of hurricane insurance. This should include a commitment to preparing homes early, lessening potential damages; enforcing a uniform building code and establishing a uniform grading system for wind resistance; providing cheaper reinsurance; encouraging innovative deductible options; and implementing stronger consumer protections. Florida will never dodge the destructive forces of Mother Nature, but these initial steps would soften the blow and lower the cost of insuring homeowners' piece of the American Dream.

CHAPTER

V

Putting Families First

"We know that when people are safe in their homes, they are free to pursue their dream for a brighter economic future for themselves and their families." George E. Pataki

Improved Access to Affordable Housing

Problem: Florida lacks affordable housing.

Floridians need affordable housing. However, due to dramatic increases in housing costs coupled with modest rises in incomes, many low- and middle-income Florida families can no longer afford safe and decent housing. Steep increases in real estate prices have also priced many middle-income families out of the market. Florida has a critical shortage of housing for those engaged in essential service occupations such as teachers, police officers, and hospital employees, thus making it increasingly difficult for many communities to recruit, employ, and retain such personnel.

Florida's affordable housing shortage is exacerbated by developers' failure to build affordable housing beyond what is legally required. This partly stems from a lack of incentives for builders to *actually construct* affordable housing. As a result, some planned housing is never built or is not constructed by the developers themselves.

Solution: Increase incentives for developers to construct affordable housing.

Florida must continue its efforts to address its affordable housing crisis. Through subsidized financing and other approaches, Florida has committed significant financial resources over the last decade to mitigate this problem. In addition, Florida's growth management laws mandate that local governments ensure the availability of adequate housing for all income groups by requiring inclusion of a housing element in each local government comprehensive plan. Such planning requirements have had mixed results.

The 2006 Legislature enacted legislation to address access to affordable housing by creating a pilot program encouraging the provision of affordable housing for essential service personnel, extending housing assistance to those with extremely low incomes, and providing other financial and regulatory incentives to encourage the provision of affordable housing. The legislation included density bonus incentives for land donations for affordable housing purposes for extremely low-income, very low-income, low-income, or moderate-income persons. Florida should increase incentives for developers to not only provide the land for affordable housing, but also construct the housing units themselves.

The House Interim Workgroup on Affordable Housing was created in August 2006 to build on past initiatives and explore other options to encourage the private sector to provide affordable housing for Floridians.

IDEA

64

IDEAS

65-67

> *"It was once said that the moral test of government is how that government treats those who are in the dawn of life, the children."* Hubert Humphrey

Protecting Florida's Children

Problem: Florida's children are in danger on the highway and on the Internet.

In the face of increasing traffic fatalities; violent, sexually charged video games and movies; online predators; and an otherwise increasingly fast-paced and dangerous environment, parents face the difficult task of protecting their children.

Between 1995 and 2004, 432 passengers were killed in automobiles operated by drivers under the age of eighteen. Florida's laws banning teenagers from driving at certain hours of the day have been effective in easing new drivers into more challenging driving situations, such as driving late at night. Florida does not, however, restrict the number of passengers that a young driver may transport. Florida must do more to protect teens and their passengers on the highways.

The Internet also poses a serious threat to Florida's children. The growing popularity of online net-working sites such as Facebook and MySpace provides online predators with easy avenues to deceive, lure, and victimize Florida's children. Users of these sites create online profiles or pages disclosing their interests, likes, dislikes, and other personal information. These profiles can be as detailed as the user chooses, and since most users feel their information is more private than it actually is, they do not usually exercise restraint. As a result, information they would not likely share with a stranger on the street is accessible with a single mouse click. Numerous sex offenders nationwide have been convicted of victimizing children they met through these sites. In 2005, the National Center for Missing and Exploited Children conducted a study of children ages ten to seventeen and found one out of seven children is solicited online. As the popularity of these sites increase, so does the danger to Florida's children.

Solution: Limit the number of passengers teen drivers are permitted to transport, and require parental verification before minors gain access to social networking websites.

To reduce distractions for teen drivers, Florida will limit the number of passengers who can be transported by drivers age eighteen and under.

To enhance child safety, Florida will require social networking sites to set up verification systems to require parental notification and consent for minors to use these sites. The consent form should detail what data is collected from users, the disclosure practices of the site operator, and what limits, if any, parents can place on their children's use of the site. Civil penalties will be enforced against anyone that falsifies or otherwise allows a minor access to the site without the proper parental notification and consent.

We will also <u>require schools to include in their codes of conduct clear instructions to students about what information is acceptable to post on such sites.</u> Schools should monitor the sites to ensure students are not posting sensitive or unacceptable material and prevent students from being exploited or endangering themselves or other students. We should take every step possible to protect our children from exploitation and harm.

"*We are stronger because we recognize that government isn't the sole answer to the most important questions, and we welcome community and faith-based organizations as partners to serve the needs of Florida families.*" Jeb Bush

Localize and Streamline the Department of Children and Families

Problem: Community-based care for foster children is enmeshed in procedural and financing regulations that hamper flexibility and impede innovation.

In 1996, the Florida Legislature launched a pilot program to redesign the child welfare system by out-sourcing foster care services to qualified service agencies led by community leaders. Under the leadership of Governor Jeb Bush, this program was expanded to include contracts with twenty-two lead agencies covering all sixty-seven counties. Funding and contract oversight remain the responsibility of the Department of Children and Families.

The development of the community-based care initiative revealed the natural tension between central accountability and local control. The early days of community-based care relied heavily on the department's central control and monitoring systems while community-based care groups (CBCs) established their systems of care and developed organizational skills and capabilities. As CBCs have gained experience, they have sought greater independence and a broader span of control. The department's successful application for a IV-E waiver allowing more flexibility in the use of federal funds for child welfare creates new opportunities for Florida to pursue innovative strategies.

The 2005 Legislature authorized a pilot program in Miami-Dade and Broward Counties to test certain changes in the roles of the department and the lead agencies. The intent of the pilot is to create a block-grant structure that establishes a fixed price contract with an independent, outcome-based evaluation. Other CBCs are also interested in participating in the pilot.

Solution: Expand the block-grant pilots authorized by the 2005 Legislature.

The primary intent of the community-based care initiative is to mobilize local communities and enlist local leaders throughout Florida to improve our child welfare system and better serve our abused, abandoned, and neglected children, including those in foster care and those awaiting adoptions. Significant progress has been made, but greater opportunities exist in the movement toward block-grant, outcome-driven operations. These programs should be modified as necessary and expanded as soon as feasible. These fundamental changes will increase community involvement, enhance efficiency through a refocusing of monitoring activities, and encourage investment in service delivery. Flexible administration of community-based care will encourage innovation and sharing of the best practices while optimizing the use of federal funds.

IDEA 68

Florida should <u>enhance independence and flexibility in community-based care.</u> This would require expansion of the pilot program in Miami-Dade and Broward counties, while similar three-year contracts should be offered to other CBCs. The Department of Children and Families, as the single state agency for child welfare services, retains overall responsibility. The pilot envisions the establishment of an independent evaluation process focusing on outcome measurement. The department and the CBCs should collaborate to develop resources for technical assistance and diffusion of best practices.

IDEA 69

Building on the idea of community empowerment, Florida should <u>create a statutory mechanism for communities to create "Children's Zones."</u> Children's Zones bring together the religious, social, educational, and recreational organizations in a disadvantaged community in order to provide a variety of activities that help children succeed. The model for this initiative is the Harlem Children's Zone. The initiative is based on two principles: first, that early intervention leads to better results; and second, that at-risk children can benefit from living in a neighborhood where a large number of adults participate with them in organized, community-based activities. Working through the CBC lead agencies, community alliances, and Healthy Families organizations, the state should support the development of such efforts in targeted neighborhoods.

By fostering a more flexible approach to the administration of state programs, including child welfare services, Florida will benefit by increasing local control and concentrating on achieving better results.

CHAPTER

VI

A Cleaner, Safer, Healthier Florida

"We shape our buildings; thereafter they shape us." Winston Churchill

Energy-Efficient Buildings Reward Program

Problem: Energy costs are rising.

Increasing energy costs hurt all utility customers. As Florida plans for its future energy needs, its growing population will require ever more electric generation capacity, which will entail additional costs for consumers. As energy costs rise, municipal utilities and consumers have much to gain from energy conservation.

Solution: Require and encourage energy efficiency.

Florida has several energy conservation programs but needs new ways to improve energy efficiency. State government must lead by example and find innovative ways to encourage consumer conservation. The 2006 Legislature enacted legislation requiring the Department of Environmental Protection to submit a report by November 1, 2006, detailing the state's leadership in energy conservation and efficiency. The report must include a description of state programs designed to achieve energy conservation and efficiency at state-owned facilities and must describe costs of implementation, program details, and current and projected energy and cost savings.

At the local level, city utilities such as Jacksonville Electric Authority (JEA) and Gainesville Regional Utilities (GRU) already have conservation programs aimed at reducing demand—partly to avoid investment in costly new power infrastructure. Energy conservation benefits the consumer through lower utility bills, higher quality of life, and a reduction in global warming.

Although energy-efficient appliances marketed under the EPA Energy STAR label have become a staple in modern homes, entirely energy-efficient homes are only now being marketed. Two federal programs exist to assist consumers in choosing energy-efficient structures by certifying them with a recognizable brand. The Energy STAR Program, administered by the Environmental Protection Agency (EPA), certifies existing homes based solely on their energy efficiency. The LEED program, run by the United States Green Building Council, not only certifies commercial buildings partly based on their EPA Energy STAR rating, but also reviews water efficiency, sustainability of the construction materials, and indoor environmental quality. Currently, the Green Building Council only certifies commercial buildings, ranking them as certified, silver, gold, or platinum, but it is in the process of finalizing a standard for residential buildings. Together, these programs encourage governments to build more efficient office buildings, while providing a marketable brand for private offices and homes.

Although LEED certifications for residential homes are still in the testing phase, Florida has begun a similar program called the Florida Green Building Standard (FGBS) that is used by both Alachua and Sarasota Counties. Both counties have ordinances providing for fast-track permits and a 50 percent reduction in building permit fees for homes that pledge to meet the FGBS. At least eighteen states currently offer incentives for new or renovated buildings that meet LEED standards. For instance, California requires all new and renovated state-owned facilities to receive, at minimum, a LEED silver rating. Other states offer incentives such as tax credits or reductions in permit fees for new private construction that meets LEED standards.

Florida should <u>implement a voluntary statewide incentive program for energy efficiency.</u> Florida should explore incentives for homes that pledge to meet the FGBS or similar standards. Increasing the energy efficiency of new homes will save homeowners money and will reduce the need for costly new electric generating facilities.

IDEA 70

Florida should <u>create an Energy Efficiency Fund to offer loans to public schools, public hospitals, cities, counties, special districts, and public care institutions.</u> Eligible projects are those with proven energy savings, such as lighting and HVAC efficiency improvements. Florida should also provide technical assistance to help customers identify ways to cut energy costs and to encourage the most efficient use of energy in their facilities. For example, Florida should help public hospitals, cities, counties, special districts, public care institutions, public K–12 school districts, nonprofit schools, hospitals, and colleges reduce energy costs in their facilities.

IDEA 71

Florida should <u>provide tax incentives to encourage homeowners and businesses to purchase energy-efficient heating, ventilation, air-conditioning, lighting, solar products, advanced metering of energy usage, windows, insulation, zone heating products, and weatherization systems.</u>

IDEA 72

IDEA 73

Furthermore, Florida will work to <u>build energy-efficient buildings that meet environmental standards and save taxpayers money.</u> As part of this initiative, appliances and energy systems with proven energy savings will be installed in new as well as existing state buildings if they can create cost savings for Florida's taxpayers. The initiative will also demonstrate the state's commitment to energy conservation and will raise public awareness of energy rating systems. As the brand names of these systems become better known, their marketability will encourage private developers to incorporate energy-efficient designs.

IDEA 74

> *"It is not book learning young men need, nor instruction about this and that, but a stiffening of the vertebrae which will cause them to be loyal to a trust, to act promptly, concentrate their energies—do the thing."*
>
> Elbert Hubbard

Environmental Gold Star Recognition

Problem: Applicants' previous permit violations are not considered when reviewing new permit applications.

Currently, the Florida Department of Environmental Protection has no comprehensive program to reward those in the regulated community who consistently meet their permit requirements. Moreover, the Department does not consistently consider applicants' past violations when reviewing requests for new permits. Requiring the Department to reward good actors by reducing red tape while focusing resources on enforcement against violators would encourage the Department to meet what should be its goal with the regulated community, namely, to efficiently and effectively protect the environment.

Solution: Institute performance-based environmental permitting.

The federal EPA runs several successful, perform-ance-based permitting programs, including the National Environmental Performance Track Program (NEPT). This program rewards top environmental performers who demonstrate environmental stewardship in various ways: for example, by setting three-year goals for continuous improvement in environmental performance or by maintaining systems to manage environmental impacts. To date, more than 400 Performance Track facilities have made 1,500 commitments to the environment. Rewards include public recognition, funding, and streamlined regulatory monitoring, reporting, and administrative procedures.

In March 2006, NEPT was recognized as a semifinalist by Harvard University for the Innovations in American Government Award. A 2005 EPA report shows twenty-one states have implemented similar programs. The efficiency of Florida's environmental staff resources and permitting duties would be increased through a reallocation of resources and innovative, efficient permitting programs such as NEPT.

IDEA

74

Florida should create a performance-based permitting program that rewards top environmental performers who demonstrate environmental stewardship with long-duration permits, automatic renewals, and shorter applications. This would send a clear message that our state supports clean industries that honor their permits. The Department of Environmental Protection should also be required to deny the permit applications of those entities that have habitually violated state environmental regulations. This would encourage good behavior from industry and send a strong message that Florida values its natural resources.

> "We must have a relentless commitment to producing a meaningful, comprehensive energy package aimed at conservation, alleviating the burden of energy prices on consumers, [and] decreasing our country's dependency on foreign oil." *Paul Gillmor*

Promote the Development of Alternative Energy Sources

Problem: Dependence on oil jeopardizes Florida's continued economic prosperity.

In his 2006 State of the Union address, President Bush declared, "Keeping America competitive requires affordable energy. And here we have a serious problem: America is addicted to oil, which is often imported from unstable parts of the world."

With recent increases in the price of gas and other energy costs, Florida's citizens are keenly aware of the nation's energy problem. Florida's economy and quality of life depend on a secure, adequate, and reliable supply of energy. As the fourth most populous state, Florida ranks third nationally in total energy consumption. As Florida's population continues to grow, so too does its demand for energy. Florida's need for electrical generation is predicted to grow by approximately 30 percent over the next ten years, while the demand for gasoline is expected to grow from the current level of more than 28 million gallons per day to 32.3 million gallons per day during the next decade.

Producing less than 1 percent of the energy it consumes and limited by its geography, Florida is more susceptible to interruptions in energy supply than any other state. Unlike other states that rely on petroleum pipelines for fuel delivery, more than 98 percent of Florida's transportation fuel arrives by sea. The state's reliance on imported petroleum products, in addition to its anticipated growth in consumption, underscores its vulnerability to fluctuations in the market and interruptions in fuel production, supply, and delivery.

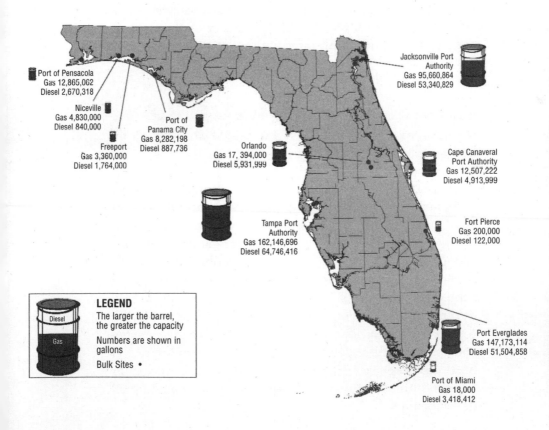

Port of Pensacola
Gas 12,865,062
Diesel 2,670,318

Niceville
Gas 4,830,000
Diesel 840,000

Freeport
Gas 3,360,000
Diesel 1,764,000

Port of Panama City
Gas 8,282,198
Diesel 887,736

Orlando
Gas 17, 394,000
Diesel 5,931,999

Tampa Port Authority
Gas 162,146,696
Diesel 64,746,416

Jacksonville Port Authority
Gas 95,660,864
Diesel 53,340,829

Cape Canaveral Port Authority
Gas 12,507,222
Diesel 4,913,999

Fort Pierce
Gas 200,000
Diesel 122,000

Port Everglades
Gas 147,173,114
Diesel 51,504,858

Port of Miami
Gas 18,000
Diesel 3,418,412

LEGEND
The larger the barrel, the greater the capacity

Numbers are shown in gallons

Bulk Sites •

Diesel

Gas

To generate electricity, Florida primarily relies on natural gas, coal, and oil imports. Together, fossil fuels represent 86 percent of Florida's total generating capacity. Less than 10 percent of its generating capacity is derived from cleaner nuclear and renewable fuels. In fact, no new nuclear plants have entered service in Florida since 1983. Current forecasts indicate that new generation capacity will be 80 percent natural gas–fired and 19 percent coal-fired. Meeting these projections could prove expensive at today's prices and lead to an over-reliance on one fuel type, affecting the reliability of electric utility generation supply in Florida. While expansions for natural gas capacity are needed and already under way, improving generation fuel diversity would enhance reliability over the long term. Too great a reliance on a single fuel source leaves Floridians subject to the risks of price volatility and supply interruption.

Solution: Promote the development and use of alternative energy sources, and begin production of ethanol.

Substitution of alternative energy sources for fossil fuels is critical to reducing our dependence on imported oil, but it will require major changes in energy technology and infrastructure and significant changes in industries such as the automobile and electric generation. Shaping national and global market forces to achieve desired change will require actions by the federal government. However, Florida has a major role to play by fostering the development and use of alternative energy sources to address specific state energy and environmental needs and concerns and to position Florida's economy to benefit from future national and international developments.

Significant steps have been taken over the last few years at both the federal and state levels to decrease reliance on imported fossil fuels. In addition, the private sector has demonstrated a strong interest in alternative energy development through significant capital investment. But much more can and must be done.

Several alternative energy sources show great promise. Solar energy and biofuels appear to be especially promising alternative energy sources for Florida. Florida has obvious advantages in the area of solar energy and is also pursuing the production of ethanol. Recent scientific developments and expected future developments could greatly expand the types of feedstock available to produce ethanol at a lower cost than that of either corn or sugar. Another promising biofuel is biodiesel, an alternative fuel that has high energy efficiency and is clean-burning. Thanks to past initiatives, Florida also appears to have achieved a leadership position in the development of hydrogen power. Clean, safe nuclear energy is another promising option to diversify Florida's energy portfolio. Other promising areas include waste-to-energy conversion and wind and water power. Florida should <u>strive to lead the nation in fostering the development and use of alternative energy sources and ethanol production.</u>

IDEA

75

With passage of SB 888 during the 2006 legislative session, Florida took steps to build on its existing initiatives to promote alternative energy development, including providing new grants, sales tax exemptions, and corporate income tax credits and adopting new nuclear power plant siting policies. In addition, the bill created the Florida Energy Commission to develop recommendations for legislation to establish a state energy policy. The commission is to file an annual report by December 31 of each year, beginning in 2007. The first report must, among other things, identify incentives for alternative energy research, development, or deployment projects.

The success of Florida's current and future initiatives will depend on several factors, including future technological developments, the development of state and national alternative energy infrastructures, and market forces. However, building on its unique conditions and recent initiatives, Florida is well positioned to lead the nation in the pursuit of alternative energy sources and should strive to achieve this goal.

> *"I feel more confident than ever that the power to save the planet rests with the individual consumer."* Denis Hayes

Fuel-Efficient Vehicle Reward Program

Problem: Fuel-efficient hybrid vehicles are too expensive.

In today's energy market, every gallon of gasoline matters. Fuel-efficient vehicles help keep money in Floridians' wallets while also reducing oil dependency. Although hybrid vehicles save on gas, Floridians find them prohibitively expensive.

Solution: Offer incentives to encourage purchases of hybrid vehicles.

Many states, Florida included, passed legislation to help consumers offset the initial price of purchasing a hybrid vehicle. And like other states, Florida currently offers hybrid vehicle owners a commuting advantage. Hybrid drivers are allowed to drive in the high-occupancy vehicle (HOV) lane at any time, regardless of their vehicle occupancy. To qualify for this exception, vehicles must be labeled in accordance with federal regulations for inherently low-emission vehicles.

Owners must also obtain a decal costing $5 or less. This HOV eligibility saves hybrid owners precious driving time and eases daily commutes.

IDEA
76

Florida should <u>offer additional incentives for clean alternative-fueled vehicles and hybrid passenger vehicles.</u> Florida should offer free and/or discounted parking and free or reduced tolls on Florida's toll roads for high fuel efficiency vehicles. Several states, including California and Maryland, have already implemented free and/or discounted parking for owners of hybrid vehicles. Baltimore and Los Angeles grant hybrid owners discounted parking in public lots, while some cities allow free parking at metered spaces, which could save residents upwards of $600 annually. Free or reduced tolls and parking are other incentives that would benefit Florida's residents and the environment. The idea would be fairly easy to implement—hybrid vehicle owners could simply obtain a special E-PASS allowing hybrid vehicles to pass through tolls at a free or discounted rate. Additionally, Florida should provide tax incentives for all clean alternative-fueled vehicles and hybrid passenger vehicles that get at least 40 miles per gallon on the highway.

Florida should explore the use of tax incentives to encourage the development and installation of devices that increase the fuel efficiency or reduce fuel consumption of existing vehicles. For example, to maintain air-conditioning or heat, long-haul truckers typically allow their trucks to idle while they are sleeping. This practice is estimated to consume over 800 million gallons of diesel fuel annually. Although special generators are available that eliminate the need for this practice, sales are slow due to their high cost. Modest tax incentives could accelerate the adoption of such technologies.

Finally, where economically feasible, Florida should <u>convert state government vehicles into a high fuel efficiency fleet.</u> Florida should require a minimum of 75 percent of state government and educational institution fleet vehicles acquired in fiscal year 2010 and thereafter, except authorized exemptions, to be biofuel or dedicated alternative-fuel vehicles or gas-electric hybrids. Furthermore, Florida should require the fleet average for cars and light-duty trucks purchased by the state to have an EPA-estimated fuel economy of at least 40 miles per gallon, or the car to have a manufacturer's estimated highway mileage rating of at least 45 miles per gallon and the light-duty truck to have a rating of at least 35 miles per gallon. Finally, Florida should provide for local governments to also transition to a high fuel efficiency fleet.

Hybrid vehicles are guaranteed to save Floridians money on gasoline while reducing emissions and helping to curb global warming. For these reasons alone, Florida should seek creative ways to entice its residents to purchase them.

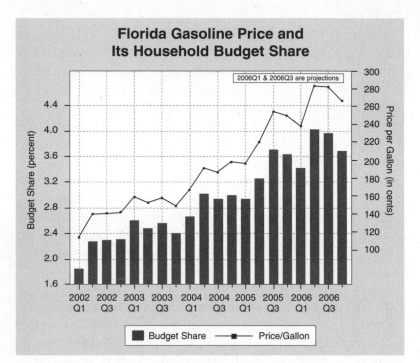

Florida Gasoline Price and Its Household Budget Share

2006Q1 & 2006Q3 are projections

Budget Share (percent)

Price per Gallon (in cents)

■ Budget Share —■— Price/Gallon

CHAPTER

VII

Quality Healthcare at an Affordable Price

> *"Medicaid is a vital safeguard for America's most needy citizens, but inefficiencies in the system are leading to inadequacies in coverage."* Paul Gillmor

Expanded Choice in Medicaid

Problem: Medicaid reform is limited to two counties, while the old program is complex, unresponsive to unique consumer needs, and costly.

For over thirty-five years, Florida's low-income families have relied on the Medicaid program for critical health services. In fiscal year 2006–2007, Florida is spending $16 billion to provide services for more than two million residents. This is more than double the $7 billion spent in 1998–1999. Despite a host of service-enhancing and cost-containing initiatives, spending and dissatisfaction among both consumers and providers continues to grow.

In 2005, after significant debate and two legislative sessions, the Legislature, with bipartisan support, authorized sweeping Medicaid reform based on Governor Bush's proposal. The new Medicaid offers consumers meaningful choices in benefits, creates incentives for wellness, and enables a variety of insurers and provider organizations to participate. Under the reform program, seventeen plans are offering innovative services to 220,000 Medicaid participants in Broward and Duval Counties. Further expansion of the program requires legislative action.

Solution: Expand Medicaid reform to empower more consumers with meaningful choices of providers and services.

The purpose of the Medicaid program is to provide access to healthcare for people with low incomes who otherwise might go without healthcare for themselves and their children. To this end, the 2005 Florida Legislature authorized a sweeping reform of the Medicaid program and directed the Agency for Health Care Administration to implement a more efficient delivery system that enhances quality of care and client outcomes. This reform began July 1, 2006, in Broward and Duval Counties, and there are plans to expand it to Baker, Clay, and Nassau Counties in the near future. With legislative approval, this reform can be expanded statewide.

The new Medicaid provides increased choices for consumers and incentives for early identification and management of chronic diseases like asthma, heart disease, and diabetes, particularly in children. Consumers have the option to choose the plans that best fit their medical needs. In addition, the new Medicaid encourages healthy habits by rewarding healthy behavior with spending accounts for health items such as over-the-counter medicine. Florida Medicaid Reform health plans will continue to offer many current Medicaid services such as vital services for children and pregnant women, hospital inpatient care, emergency care, outpatient surgery, prescription drugs, and more.

Medicaid reform modifies the financing system to ensure appropriate levels of financial support to meet patients' needs. More money is provided for consumers who have more significant healthcare needs. Initially, reform participants are those in two eligibility categories—low-income families and persons who are elderly and disabled. The remaining Medicaid patients should be able to benefit from the reform initiative as soon as possible. A critical step in this process is the development of a risk-adjusted rate structure inclusive of both medical and home and community-based services. With this step, truly coordinated systems of care can develop.

Even with legislative action to encourage statewide implementation, preliminary steps are important for the effective adoption of this model statewide. Reform relies on capitated managed care systems to achieve fiscal accountability and better value for patients. While HMOs are important participants in the reform process, the plan also invites active provider participation through the development of provider service networks (PSNs), an innovative method of service delivery in which providers offer expertise in care management. The Medicaid program should work with newly formed PSNs to ensure a variety of choices for consumers.

Florida should give Medicaid participants control over their own health while encouraging healthy habits. Medicaid reform encourages individuals to make healthy decisions by rewarding those choices with credits in enhanced benefit accounts used to purchase health-related over-the-counter items at participating pharmacies. In the initial phase, the maximum credit will be $125 per year. This incentive for healthy behavior should be expanded by increasing the total value of available credits and the types of services that can be purchased with these credits.

IDEA
78

The Medicaid reform initiated by Governor Bush and the 2005 Legislature seeks to do more than tinker with the current system; it reinvents the way healthcare is provided and financed. This means ending paternalistic and centralized decision-making on behalf of Medicaid patients. Empowering consumers with meaningful choices and stimulating continuous improvement in quality requires that providers be allowed to find new ways to improve service through more flexible plans.

IDEAS
79-80

> *"Our challenges are not marginal and their solutions are not incremental. The sooner we get honest about those facts, the sooner we can get on with the job."*
>
> Donald M. Berwick, M.D.

Value-Based Financial Support for Florida's Hospitals

Problem: Tax support for Florida's hospitals is uneven, and public subsidies may support inefficient hospital operations.

Florida licenses 280 acute care and specialty hospitals. These facilities are generally classified in three ownership categories: public, private non-profit, and investor-owned. However, these groupings fail to convey the complexity of ownership arrangements and the mixture of public and private resources used to support hospital care. Management contracts and other forms of public-private partnerships complicate the ownership landscape. Public support for hospitals flows through Medicare and Medicaid coverage of eligible recipients, local tax supports, and various forms of service-specific subsidies. Florida communities offer differing amounts and types of local tax support, while hospitals provide various kinds and scopes of services to indigent and charity patients. With all these variations in form, function, and financing, it is nearly impossible to determine whether the result is fair to Florida taxpayers and prudent for Florida's patients.

Hospitals contribute to the public good in two primary ways: first, they offer essential medical services to meet community needs; and second, they provide services to uninsured and low-income patients even when these individuals cannot afford the care. To continue meeting these important public needs, hospitals rely on various forms of public support and subsidies. The most common form of support is Medicare and Medicaid coverage that pays for individual care and also provides additional supplemental payments. In Florida, Medicaid distributes more than $1 billion in payments to hospitals through its Medicaid Low Income Pool and disproportionate share program.

Various forms of local tax support are also available, such as the establishment of tax districts. Dependent tax districts derive their revenue from ad valorem taxes when such levies are approved by their respective county commissions. Independent districts have authority to levy taxes without the additional approval of the county, although in many cases local referenda must initially approve the tax. The governing bodies of tax districts can be appointed or elected. The structure of each district depends on its local charter, which is codified in state law. Millage rates are set locally and vary from district to district. Although hospital tax districts generally rely on property taxes, counties are also authorized to levy sales tax surcharges to support healthcare.

Scope of services, patterns of utilization, quality of care, and operations efficiency vary widely among hospitals that receive public subsidies as well as those that do not. Tax support for hospitals is not spent in a way that promotes value. Some publicly funded hospitals may deliver value (defined as efficient, quality care), but we have not created a financial framework that consistently generates improved efficiency and outcomes.

Solution: Develop the infrastructure for value-based competition in providing publicly funded hospital services.

Measuring patient care results is the first step in building a healthcare system that persistently improves cost effectiveness. Consequently, Florida should develop a system to measure care results for specific medical conditions and require hospitals to participate in reporting as a condition of receiving public funds. We should then use the result measurements to assess value delivered by publicly funded providers, thus ensuring that tax dollars help improve outcomes for patients.

Value-based competition, as described in *Redefining Health Care*, is a powerful vision to transform today's dysfunctional competition into a system that rewards good results without micromanaging facilities or second-guessing the clinical judgment of providers. The authors call for a realignment of fundamental incentives by making value—that is, patient outcomes per unit of cost—the focal point of financing decisions. They argue that competition should be centered on the results produced for patients over a full cycle of care for specific medical conditions.

In the current system, public financing for hospital services is linked to specific institutions or geopolitical entities, and the primary goal of public spending is to protect the financial viability of those entities. Value-based competition, in contrast, calls for spending decisions to reward providers that achieve the best patient outcomes. Such a fundamental change in the way tax funding supports healthcare requires basic changes to the organization and delivery of healthcare. Publicly funded providers, including hospitals in tax districts chartered in state law as well as other tax-exempt hospitals, can lead this transformation, particularly if they provide significant care to the uninsured.

IDEA

79

Florida should secure accountability for quality and costs from hospitals receiving tax support. This approach requires a redefinition of business goals, careful assessment of services and functions, systematic improvement of processes, and development of the capacity to measure results. The state should pilot this initiative by creating the opportunity for providers to voluntarily participate in "Enterprise Zones." An Enterprise Zone is a deregulated catchment area in which all hospitals (both those already in the community and any new hospitals opening in the area) make two important commitments to the public good: first, they agree to participate in the collection, analysis, and comparison of patient value; and second, they commit to either provide or pay for a specified amount of healthcare for uninsured Floridians. The exemptions available in the Enterprise Zone should include freedom from market-entry and other government regulations so long as essential protections for public health and safety are retained.

Another way Florida could maximize state resources while ensuring efficient, high-quality healthcare would be to evaluate outsourcing the management and operation of all state-owned hospitals. The evaluation process will enable the state to streamline and modernize the management and operation of these institutions. The state has already realized savings and service improvements from the privatization of South Florida State Hospital, a 350-bed psychiatric hospital. Another facility, the South Florida Evaluation and Treatment Center, was slated for privatization in 2005. The state, however, continues to operate several facilities, including a 100-bed specialty hospital for tuberculosis, three institutions for persons with severe and persistent mental illness, and three facilities for persons with significant developmental disabilities. Florida should improve efficiency and performance at state-owned and operated facilities by evaluating outsourcing and other potential operational changes.

IDEA

80

> *"Health is the first of all liberties."*
> Henri Amiel

Coordinated Care for Florida's Seniors

Problem: Long-term care is fragmented and lacks sufficient incentives for appropriate placement and use of home and community care.

Florida has the highest 65+ population percentage in the nation and the fourth-highest proportion of persons age eighty-five and older. Of the three million seniors living in Florida, over one million have at least one type of disability. Many of these disabilities, while hampering self-care, can be managed using home and community-based services.

Family members provide the vast majority of long-term care services assisting elders with daily activities and basic needs. When needs exceed the abilities and resources of family members, services are sought from paid providers. Few elders have insurance coverage for long-term care, and these services can be costly. As a result, many seniors depend on publicly funded programs including a variety of services offered through the Department of Elder Affairs and the Medicaid program.

In 2006–2007, Florida will provide $4.3 billion in Medicaid funding for long-term care.

Despite extensive efforts to promote home and community-based care over the last two decades, significant obstacles remain to ensuring that Florida's seniors receive the care they need in the least restrictive environment possible. The principal barriers are eligibility limits and the fragmentation of services, which can confuse the elderly. Florida Senior Care is designed to provide an integrated system of long-term care services in order to promote the use of community care and enhance service quality.

Solution: Implement Florida Senior Care.

For more Florida seniors to remain independent and receive the care they need at home and in their communities, Florida should implement Florida Senior Care—a program that utilizes systems of coordinated care—to provide all Medicaid services for eligible participants. The plan includes physician services, prescription drugs, hospitalization, durable medical equipment, transportation, mental health services, and a variety of home care services. This initiative builds on Florida's experience with managed long-term care through the nursing home diversion waiver.

IDEA
81

The nursing home diversion program is fully capitated for almost all Medicaid services, including Medicare co-pays and deductibles, home and community-based services, and, if needed, nursing home care. Although generally successful, the program is limited by the high frailty criteria that restrict eligibility. While this restriction ensures the program enrolls the most needy, it also increases the financial risk for the managed care plan and denies the use of preventive and other support services before frailty advances.

Florida Senior Care is intended to promote community-based long-term care services, manage health costs, coordinate care, and establish accountability for patient outcomes. The project will streamline eligibility determinations and develop new quality management systems. Integrated service networks will develop at the local level in response to program incentives that emphasize community care.

This program will give enrolled seniors access to a coordinated and comprehensive system of care that enables them to maintain their independence longer. They will be able to choose the plan that best suits their needs, and gain access to a care coordinator who helps them to navigate the service delivery system as their needs change.

The Agency for Health Care Administration has received waiver approval from the federal government to implement the program, which requires the further approval of the Florida Legislature.

> *"I am a firm believer in the people. If given the truth, they can be depended upon to meet any national crisis. The great point is to bring them the real facts."* Abraham Lincoln

Use Transparency to Foster Value-Based Healthcare Decisions

Problem: Current transparency initiatives are limited to specific procedures and do not support comparative evaluations of providers based on value to patients.

Florida took important first steps toward transparency with the passage of HB 1629 in 2004. In this bill, the Legislature directed the Agency for Health Care Administration to develop a system to provide information on the cost, utilization, and quality of healthcare services. FloridaCompareCare.com was launched in 2005, making Florida the first state to offer a website evaluating the performance of hospitals, ambulatory care centers, physicians, and pharmacies.

Consumers using FloridaCompareCare can find utilization, quality, and cost data on a large number of healthcare providers in the state. For instance, the website reports quality indicators such as risk-adjusted mortality, readmission rates, infection rates, bedsore rates, complication rates, and other indicators for any hospital in Florida. The results of such queries inform consumers whether the selected indicator was lower, higher, or as expected after adjusting for risk and comparing to the state average. This website is an important first step, but it must evolve into a more user-friendly source of information helping consumers to find the providers who deliver the best results for their medical conditions.

Take, for example, patients with heart problems who want to know which provider offers the best cardiac care. FloridaCompareCare offers a myriad of data on this question. But its usefulness is hampered by the data's narrowness (in terms of readmissions, complications and mortality by procedure, and complaints), the fragmented presentation of the information, and the limitations of the standard of measurement. The website offers extensive information on heart attacks, but it is unlikely to be useful during an actual heart attack. Furthermore, it fails to reveal which provider achieves better outcomes over a full cycle of care for cardiac patients.

Solution: Enhance FloridaCompareCare to provide consumers with comparative information on the results of care for specific medical conditions.

Florida is making progress toward publicly reporting healthcare information through FloridaCompare Care, but we must do better. Advancing to the next stage of transparency requires additional infrastructure. We must define new bases for analysis that are meaningful to consumers. This will require more data from more providers and a capacity to track patient care through time in order to assess a full cycle of care, not just the immediate result of a specific intervention. We must establish new measures for medical care that allow for meaningful comparisons of expertise and results for specific medical conditions.

Florida should <u>reward healthcare providers and plans that demonstrate better outcomes at lower cost.</u> This program can begin by focusing on a few common conditions like diabetes, chronic kidney care, and cardiac care, and establish appropriate measures of value based on patients' results over a full cycle of care offered by an integrated unit of service providers. Award candidates would have to submit data to be evaluated and compared to one another. The awards, like the MacArthur "genius" awards, should be substantial and come without strings in order to inspire and reward the diligent work of providers toward improving value for patients.

IDEA 82

Transparency is a critical component for building a more efficient healthcare system in Florida. The state can take a number of short-term steps to make more effective use of technology for meeting patients' healthcare needs. Many pharmaceutical manufacturers offer programs to assist low-income and uninsured patients to gain access to needed medications. Finding these programs and navigating through different qualifying procedures can be challenging and time-consuming. Florida should <u>create a "one-stop" source of information on assistance for Florida's uninsured.</u>

IDEA 83

Florida's Medicaid program has initiated strategies to encourage physicians to use e-prescribing to promote better patient care and to avoid prescription errors. Florida should <u>reward physicians who use technology like e-prescribing to reduce errors and improve efficiency.</u>

IDEA 84

The Florida Health Information Network is the initiative begun under Governor Bush's leadership to develop a comprehensive, integrated system of privacy-protected health records. The purpose of this network is to enhance point-of-care availability of medical information, provide decision support systems to health-care providers, and assist public health functions of monitoring and disease reporting. Florida should <u>improve patient care through technology by expanding electronic health records and regional health information networks.</u> This concept necessitates a technical infrastructure for electronic health records that is confidential, interoperable, and transmittable in real time via the Internet.

> *"America enjoys the best healthcare in the world, but the best is no good if folks can't afford it, access it, and doctors can't provide it."* Bill Frist

Accountable, Accessible Healthcare

Problem: More than three million Floridians lack health insurance and may face barriers in accessing needed health services.

Currently, 19.2 percent of Florida residents, or 3.4 million people, lack health insurance. While numerous important safety net programs offer care to the uninsured, health insurance remains the most common means for securing needed health services. People who have health insurance are more likely to obtain routine and preventive care and to access timely intervention for serious health problems.

Lack of health insurance does not uniformly affect all Floridians. Medicare covers people age sixty-five and older, while Medicaid covers those with very low incomes and with disabilities. Most of the uninsured are working-aged adults, about two-thirds of whom have a paying job. At least one-third of the state's uninsured live in South Florida (including Miami-Dade and Broward Counties). Over 30 percent of Hispanics and 23 percent of African

Americans are uninsured. Employment-based health insurance is the most common source of coverage, but many small employers do not offer insurance, a trend that is increasing. Nearly 70 percent of the working uninsured reported their employers did not offer coverage in 2004.

In 2004 the Florida Health Insurance Study found that 12.1 percent of children under the age of nineteen, or 534,000 children, are uninsured in Florida. While this finding represents a drop in the rate of uninsurance since 1999, the number of uninsured children remains a concern. A majority of these children live in families with incomes below 200 percent of the federal poverty level and would qualify for Florida Healthy Kids, a state program primarily funded by the federal State Children's Health Insurance Program (SCHIP).

Florida Healthy Kids enrollment has dropped by over 130,000 from its peak several years ago, primarily due to the tightening of eligibility screening procedures. Consequently, Florida has underspent its federal SCHIP allocations by more than $450 million. Because of lagging enrollment, the Legislature reduced funding for Healthy Kids by about $170 million. Based on current enrollment, Florida will underspend its annual FFY 2007 allotment by about $100 million. Congress is set to reauthorize SCHIP next year for FFY 2008 and beyond. If Florida does not map out a concrete plan to increase enrollment in Florida Healthy Kids, the state may lose funds to other states that regularly spend their annual block grant.

Expansion of government subsidies for health insurance or health services must be accomplished in a fiscally responsible manner. With typical family insurance premiums averaging $11,000 per year, the cost of sponsoring additional coverage or investing in more services is likely to be staggering. Other states have spread these costs through employer and individual mandates, but these approaches violate fundamental principles of limited government.

Solution: Increase access to affordable health insurance and enhance support for safety net programs.

A variety of programs and services exist to meet the healthcare needs of low-income and uninsured residents. These efforts include Florida KidCare, the Florida Health Insurance Plan, HealthFlex, community-based free clinics, and other safety net programs. The state should expand these efforts, but the first step is a thorough accounting of current programs and spending. Floridians should know what healthcare programs and services are available to the uninsured and how taxpayer money is used to support these initiatives.

By addressing Florida's uninsured, the Legislature will simultaneously protect Floridians' health and limit the negative economic impact the uninsured have on the state. The state's investment will produce a valuable return by avoiding many preventable illnesses and constraining the rate of growth in spending for healthcare.

Florida should make it easier for qualified, uninsured children to get coverage through Florida KidCare. This streamlining would cover many of the uninsured children at minimal state cost. The federal SCHIP program pays seventy-one cents of every dollar spent on eligible children. With expected costs at about $120 per member per month in Florida KidCare, Florida can offer comprehensive healthcare coverage, with minimal family premiums and co-pays, to children at less than $35 per month per child in state dollars.

IDEA

86

Florida should <u>launch a marketplace of affordable health insurance.</u> This will facilitate comparison and competition among private sector plans that would be exempt from statutory mandates on health insurance coverage. Without mandates, insurers and HMOs will be free to offer innovative coverage plans. For example, niche plans for people with specific conditions featuring disease management services and a limited drug formulary might be offered, or high-deductible plans paired with health savings accounts might be attractive to some consumers. The role of the state would be to offer information, a consistent framework for comparison, and limited choice counseling to consumers. To further jump-start this program, the state could also provide a partial subsidy for a limited number of qualified subscribers. In this way, the state can offer a defined investment in healthcare coverage in order to improve the public health and reduce uncompensated care.

More employers should be encouraged to offer coverage to their employees. The state should provide incentives to employers such as eliminating requirements for workers' compensation for employers that offer health and short-term disability insurance.

<u>Providers should be encouraged to expand preventive services and walk-in care for uninsured Floridians.</u> For example, pharmacists could improve access to preventive care if they were allowed to offer flu shots. This strategy removes an unnecessary limitation on their scope of practice and offers an easy and accessible way for patients to be protected from communicable diseases. Special tax waivers for physicians and clinics who provide this care might enable them to earn relief from the sales tax on selected items such as medical equipment and supplies. Furthermore, many communities have developed

free clinics and utilized the services of retired health professionals. The process for obtaining necessary licenses for these retired practitioners and for securing sovereign immunity should be simplified. We should make it easy for providers to help the uninsured.

Florida should assist hospitals in helping patients with immediate medical problems to avoid emergency departments while still receiving the necessary care.

**Percent of uninsured Floridians under age 65
by age category, 1999 and 2004**

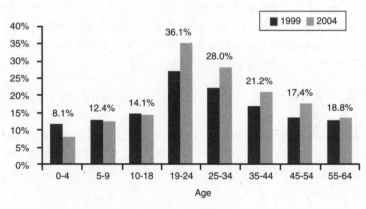

2004 Florida Health Insurance Study (FHIS)

Opportunity and Prosperity for the Next Generation

> *"In this world of change, some things do not change: the values we try to live by, the institutions that give our lives meaning and purpose. Our society rests on a foundation of responsibility and character and family commitment."* George W. Bush

Create a Family-Friendly Hollywood in Florida

Problem: Florida has failed to enact a long-term investment strategy for the film and entertainment industry.

Florida's film industry has an enormous economic impact on the state's economy. A 2003 economic assessment by Economics Research Associates showed that the core motion picture production industry employed 8,492 wage and salary workers, providing over $372 million in wages to Florida workers in 2001. In addition, for every dollar invested in Florida's film incentive program, there is a direct return on investment of $6.71. Yet Florida has failed to enact a long-term investment strategy for this industry. At an idearaiser in August 2006, many ideas were proposed to improve Florida's presence in the entertainment industry and to lure more film and television producers to our state.

The current film incentive operates within two queues and is dispensed on a first-come, first-served basis. According to Florida law, 60 percent of funds provided for the film incentive goes into Queue One—feature films, TV movies, commercials, music videos, industrial or educational films, promotional films, documentaries, TV specials, and digital media–effects productions. The remaining 40 percent goes into Queue Two—TV pilots and TV series (dramas, comedies, reality, telenovela, soaps, game shows, miniseries, etc.). Each production must spend a minimum of $850,000 in the state to qualify for the film incentive.

In the past two years, not one commercial or music video has qualified for Florida's film incentive. In addition, by the time the industry is ready to consider filming television pilots in the early spring, the incentives have typically been earmarked for other productions. TV series are especially critical to our state's workforce because a series provides years of employment, whereas a film lasts only a few months. Another major problem is timing. Productions, especially higher-budget ones, must plan their filming schedule months to a year in advance. When considering filming in Florida, they do not have assurances from the state that the film incentive will be funded the following year.

Solution: Establish the film industry as a priority industry in Florida.

Currently, Florida invests in its film industry on an annual basis. Last year, the incentive program was funded at $10 million; this year the program was increased to $20 million. However, an annual appropriation provides no long-term commitment to this important industry, thus diminishing Florida's ability to compete with other states. Florida should create a tax incentive program aimed at attracting more film production and TV series to the state, with priority given to those productions that are given "family-friendly" ratings such as G or PG. Such a tax incentive program will ensure long-term sta-

IDEA
90

bility and investment in the film and entertainment industry. Providing tax credits for a specified number of years will allow productions to plan ahead with the certainty that the incentive will be available. Expanding the tax credit or providing a tax rebate to family friendly–rated productions would further promote Florida's commitment to family values. Additionally, such an incentive program will allow productions to develop filming schedules without being hindered by the end of the state's fiscal year.

Providing four separate queues—1) film, television, and episodic; 2) commercial and video; 3) TV pilots; and 4) independent film—will allow more of the industry to participate in the incentive and will increase production in the state by attracting more commercials and TV series to Florida.

Lowering the minimum expenditure will allow the state to attract more commercials, TV pilots, and independent films to Florida. The current Screen Actors Guild recommends a $625,000 threshold.

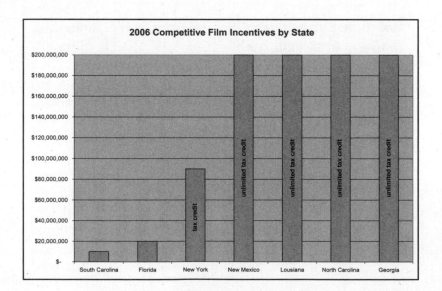

IDEA 91

> *"Entrepreneurs and their small enterprises are responsible for almost all the economic growth in the United States."* Ronald Reagan

Business Development

Problem: Florida is at a competitive disadvantage with other states in investing in new business development.

Early stage and seed capital is critical to Florida's success, particularly as Florida's R&D community accelerates its cutting-edge ideas for the marketplace. At present, a number of Florida's innovations are going unfunded or are commercialized out of state. Idearaiser participants identified the need for incentives to encourage business development.

Solution: Invest in early stage venture capital as the fuel to turn good ideas into new growth companies and high-wage jobs.

More than being a center for innovation, Florida needs to create a mechanism to help Florida technologies and ideas develop into Florida-based companies. Florida will establish a nationally recognized business investment program to encourage creation of more high-wage jobs for Floridians. Creation of a transferable and tradable tax credit program would act

IDEA

91

as a guarantee for private investment in early-stage venture capital to support Florida's R&D industry.

The availability of local seed capital will fill a major void, getting incipient, R&D-intensive companies through the crucial stage of idea creation to product development and growth. The successful encouragement of private investment in Florida technologies will lead to the creation of new companies and new high-wage jobs. Florida will also attract the attention of large national venture capital funds.

Entrepreneurial-driven commercialization is key to diversifying Florida's economy, and venture capital is crucial for that commercialization to occur. In general, the venture capital industry currently focuses on later-stage investments with clear exit strategies, primarily in a few regions of the United States, excluding Florida. A key factor to successfully bringing innovation to the marketplace will be the presence of local seed capital:

- 75 percent of all venture deals are done within fifty miles of the venture capital firm's office.

- Post 9/11, people are less willing to spend time on airplanes, and traveling to Florida from the Northeast or West Coast for meetings is a two-day trip.

- Early stage deals require a lot of hand-holding. Administrative and logistical concerns are minimized when local venture capital is invested in local projects.

The availability of local venture capital will lead to other successes, attracting the attention and interest of nationwide investors and larger venture funds.

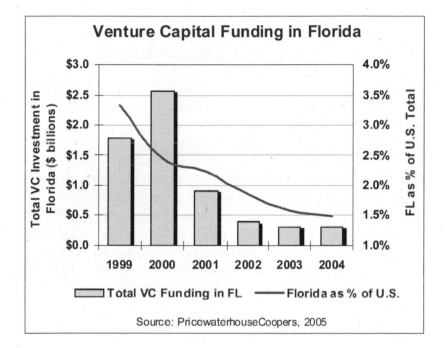

> *"Frivolous lawsuits are booming in this country. The U.S. has more costs of litigation per person than any other industrialized nation in the world, and it is crippling our economy."* Jack Kingston

Loser Pays for Frivolous Lawsuits

Problem: Frivolous litigation is increasing.

The litigious nature of society as a whole is undeniable. The high cost of ever-present frivolous lawsuits in our society led citizens to submit ideas to the 100ideas website and to idearaisers across the state. A common problem with previous proposed solutions is that they could harm those who legitimately seek redress. Defense against any accusation, with or without merit, is expensive.

The Florida Rules of Civil Procedure have greatly expanded discovery in order to enhance parties' ability to discover relevant facts and test the strength of their cases. Through seemingly limitless depositions, exhaustive requests for production, and extensive interrogatories, a party to a lawsuit spends months and thousands of dollars in the discovery process alone. Frequently, a lawsuit becomes a continuous discovery battle with little or no chance of

Litigation blackmail must be stopped.

resolution based on the merits. The rules are often abused by plaintiffs and defendants alike.

The Florida Legislature created a substantive right to attorneys' fees for litigation in certain circumstances. In 1999, section 57.105, Florida Statutes was amended to mandate the award of fees when parties were found to have either brought claims or defended against claims with arguments not supported by the facts or suitable evidence. This amendment abolished "frivolous" as a relevant concept when determining eligibility for fees, and also made attorneys and clients each responsible for paying half of any awarded fees.

Attorneys can avoid shared responsibility for fees by demonstrating a reasonable reliance on a factual scenario presented by a client, in which case the client is solely liable for any fees. Although attorneys can be relieved of their half of a fee award due to fanciful facts provided by a client, there is no relief provided for clients who show reasonable reliance on an attorney's capricious legal representations.

The Legislature additionally entered the offer of judgment statute in chapter 768. This provision sought to encourage settlements by crafting a substantive right to attorneys' fees when a reasonable settlement offer was refused. The statute uses the final result of a case to measure the reasonableness of any previous offer, provides time for considering an offer, and allows a fairly broad margin to measure success.

A problem with this area of the law is the rule adopted by the Florida Supreme Court to implement the statute. The rule has created obligations the statute does not impose, and in many instances it denies substantive rights the Legislature has granted. Rules of procedure should never be construed to deny substantive rights granted by the Legislature.

The Legislature has also enacted several "loser pays" or "prevailing party" statutes including chapter 448—the whistleblowers statute. Statutes also impose liability for a prevailing party's attorneys' fees only on an identified party, such as an insurance company in a policy dispute, pursuant to chapter 667. Another example is workers' compensation, in which successful claimants are awarded attorneys' fees based on the value of benefits their attorneys obtain on their behalf. Both of these types of "loser pays" or "prevailing party" statutes should be expanded.

Solution: Clarify and expand mechanisms sanctioning those that pursue meritless or needless litigation.

To reduce the number of meritless lawsuits, the Legislature will expand the "loser pays" or "prevailing party" attorneys' fee statutes, strengthen the "offer of judgment" statute, and ensure that any case, claim, or defense not supported by necessary facts or law results in the right to claim attorneys' fees. Reducing the ability to pursue meritless litigation by increasing its cost is a simple economic solution; if the loser has to assume the cost of litigation for both sides, those seeking damages will be more cautious. As for expanded "loser-pays" or "prevailing party" statutes, these may be imposed within a court's discretion, similar to the whistleblowers act.

IDEA 92

Additionally, the offer of judgment statute (section 768.79) provides a way for litigants to settle a case for its value without additional cost for attorneys' fees. The statute allows a party to offer a settlement and gives the opposing party thirty days to accept or reject it. The prospect of the imposition of attorneys' fees acts as an incentive to accept. However rule 1.442, implementing the offer of judgment statute, not only imposes unduly burdensome requirements on the offeror, but it also has been interpreted in a manner that frustrates the purpose of the statute. The statute should therefore be amended to specify the following points: the award of attorneys' fees is a substantive right granted by the Legislature that cannot be abolished by the courts; the recipient of a settlement offer has the burden of clarifying any uncertainties in an offer's terms or conditions; an offer to joint parties need not be itemized as separate offers if the liability of one party is derivative of the liability of the others; an offer may be made at any time for any amount by any party; a party will be bound by its offer if it is accepted, regardless of that party's level of knowledge about the case; and zero or nominal offers cannot be evaluated to determine "good-faith."

The 1999 amendments to section 57.105 helped address the problem of abusive litigation. However, the statute should be amended to clarify that "frivolous" is not the relevant criteria for determining entitlement to fees. Any case, claim, or defense not supported by necessary facts or law should result in the substantive right to an award of attorneys' fees. Furthermore, courts should have the authority to order fees from attorneys who mislead their clients about the law.

IDEAS

93-95

Give Citizens Greater Control over Government Taxing and Spending Policies

Problem: Governmental entities can too easily increase taxes and spending.

Florida has the seventh-lowest unemployment rate in the country and leads the nation in job growth. This is influenced in part by conservative budget practices and limited government spending. Over the past eight years, government has cut state and local taxes and fees by $19.3 billion. When the budget ran a surplus, some of the excess cash balances were set aside as reserves, expected to total $6.5 billion at the end of this fiscal year. Additionally, excess revenues were used conservatively to prevent undue growth in recurring spending. These fiscal practices, however, are only informal, subject to budgetary approval and the views of whoever occupies the Legislature and the governor's office.

However, not all local governments have practiced fiscal restraint. With the recent rise in housing prices, local governments have seen property taxes increase by 80 percent in six years, compared to 39 percent growth in personal income over the same period. Despite the property boom, recent findings from the Auditor General identify financial trends indicating deteriorating financial conditions. Typically, local governments resolve such a situation by raising taxes.

Currently, sixteen states require certain forms of tax hikes to pass by supermajorities of either three-fifths, two-thirds, or three-fourths in both legislative chambers. Other than requiring a three-fifths supermajority to increase the corporate income tax, Florida can increase taxes on a simple majority vote.

State and local taxes matter to the businesses that employ our residents. Tax competition between states for jobs is nothing new. Within America's fifty-state free trade zone, lawmakers have long known that their states' tax structures affect their competitiveness with neighbors. In today's increasingly mobile world, low-tax states are lining up to poach companies away from high-tax states. In light of the growth of Florida's population and economy, we must ensure that our tax system does not become overly burdensome to residents and remains welcoming to incoming businesses.

Solution: Maintain a business-friendly tax environment.

A business-friendly tax environment is crucial to the economic well-being of a state and its citizens. Florida's continuing position as a national leader in job creation highlight the connection between job growth and low corporate taxes. Florida, with an unemployment rate of just 3.3 percent, added 259,800 jobs (seasonally adjusted) from July 2005 to July 2006, contributing to a. job growth rate that more than doubles the national average. Florida is ranked forty-ninth in state government expenditures and thirty-second in per capita state and local taxes, according to Florida TaxWatch and the U.S. Census bureau.

To protect, and potentially enhance, Florida's business-friendly tax environment, government at all levels needs to act prudently in expenditures and modes of taxation. Since the benefits of this approach cannot reasonably be disputed, the Legislature should carefully protect it.

Florida should <u>adopt a constitutional amendment prohibiting its governments from growing faster than the incomes of their taxpaying citizens.</u> This amendment will establish revenue limits for both state and local governments, requiring revenues exceeding those limits to be returned to taxpayers through tax relief or used for improving infrastructure or schools in high-growth areas. Further, it would limit state budget growth each year by linking it to the rate of inflation and population growth, and prevent local governments from raising property and other taxes. Revenue limitations have already proven effective elsewhere; the thirty states that have revenue limitations have seen an average of 17.4 percent employment growth and 68.7 percent personal income growth in ten years, compared to 13.7 percent and 64 percent growth respectively for states without limitations. The sixteen states with some type of tax limitations have enjoyed similar advantages in employment and income growth over the states that lack them. For Florida, limited spending and low taxes will continue to drive economic growth. Establishing revenue limits and guidelines will help Florida's governments effectively manage their budgets while protecting citizens from unnecessary tax increases.

Florida should also <u>require a supermajority vote for any tax increases.</u> According to a Heritage Foundation study, states with supermajority requirements reaped a myriad of benefits and had slower growth of tax and spending rates. Furthermore, the economies in supermajority states grew almost one-third faster and employment rose approximately 25 percent faster than in other states. Further tax constrains would control the growth of government and force legislative discipline over budget and tax practices, resulting in more responsible spending of taxpayer dollars. Clearly, the likely benefits far outweigh any potential downside in supermajority voting for tax hikes, which will effectively reinforce the principles of efficient and accountable state government.

Florida will <u>reduce the tax on phone, cable, cellular, and satellite services.</u> Florida's state and local taxes on communications are among the nation's highest, averaging over 13 percent for most services. These taxes should be cut, since these services are more a necessity than a luxury for most Florida families and businesses. Bringing these taxes in line with the general sales tax will make the tax system more fair and enhance Florida's overall economic environment. The longevity of communications taxes is highly uncertain anyway, given rapid technological advances and the increasing use of the Internet.

> *"In times of growth, tax dollars should be returned to working families and small businesses in Florida. We must remember that tax dollars belong to our citizens, not the government."* Jeb Bush

Constitutionally Eliminate or Cap Skyrocketing Property Taxes

Problem: The property tax system is inequitable.

Aside from the high cost of homeowners' insurance, no idea was raised more frequently in the 100idea process than the need to curb the meteoric rise in property taxes. Florida is one of only nine states without a state personal income tax and has a reputation for being a low-tax, fiscally sound state. However, since 2000 Florida's property tax burden has been growing disproportionately faster than personal income. That means Floridians are dedicating more of their hard-earned money to property taxes than ever before. Prices for housing and commercial properties have been skyrocketing in Florida. For the last four years, property values have grown at double-digit rates. Consequently, property taxes increased 28 percent in the ten years following 1994, when Florida implemented a voter-approved initiative to cap property taxes called Save Our Homes. Since growing property tax values have not been offset by declining property tax rates, the total dollar value of property taxes paid has increased dramatically.

Just prior to the Save Our Homes initiative, property tax levies comprised $36–$38 per $1,000 of personal income in Florida. Following the initiative's implementation, the tax burden initially remained largely unchanged, amounting to $35.44 in 1995. The tax burden then steadily declined through 2000 and subsequently increased rapidly through 2005 to over $43.48. Over this entire eleven-year period, property taxes grew by 10 percent while personal income grew by only 6.7 percent.

Businesses, which are not covered by the Save Our Homes exemption, have borne a disproportionately large portion of the higher property tax burden. These costs are then passed on to hardworking Florida consumers.

Solution: Constitutionally eliminate or cap property taxes.

The backbone of good government is financial accountability. County governments are responsible for raising the necessary revenues to finance a variety of critical, basic public services, yet have a duty to tax residents at a reasonable rate. Therefore, Florida will amend the constitution to either place caps on all property taxes or, alternatively, abolish the property tax in whole or in part.

IDEA 96

The options include eliminating the property tax on homestead properties, increasing the homestead exemption to the median home price, and placing a 3 percent annual cap on non-homestead properties.

Eliminating or curbing property taxes will lead to an immediate increase in housing affordability, help boost the value of Florida homes, and keep government fiscally accountable. Lower property taxes will help renters too, as lower costs for landlords will lead to a decrease in rents throughout the state. By eliminating or capping the property tax, we also eliminate a significantly rising cost for businesses, which will be able to cut their pre–sales tax prices if they pay less for their property or leased space. With more income to spend (and save), total spending in Florida will increase. Property values will continue to rise and businesses will have less overhead costs, allowing them to pass along savings to consumers.

In place of property taxes, the state sales tax rate should be adjusted, after voter approval, to replace lost revenues. The sales tax is a good revenue source for Florida because it is a flat tax that does not discourage job and economic growth. The increase in the sales tax would be limited by the baby boomer generation and tourist consumer groups. As boomers prepare to retire, this policy will draw more of them to Florida, where they will spend a generation's worth of retirement savings estimated at $400 billion. Additionally, due to the large tourist industry in Florida, residents from other states or countries would pay a sizeable portion of this tax.

Eliminating or capping the property tax will mitigate numerous difficult costs that affect Floridians every day. Thanks to this bold reform, the Legislature and local governments, working as partners, both stand to benefit by re-examining each other's roll in taxing, but more importantly, Florida residents will enjoy a higher quality of life at a more reasonable price.

Florida Personal Income Growth vs. Property Tax Revenue Growth

Year-on-Year Growth (1990–2005)

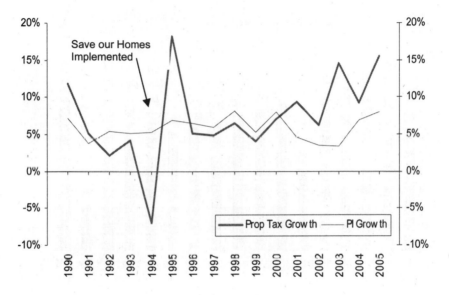

Total Florida Property Taxes per $1,000 of Personal Income

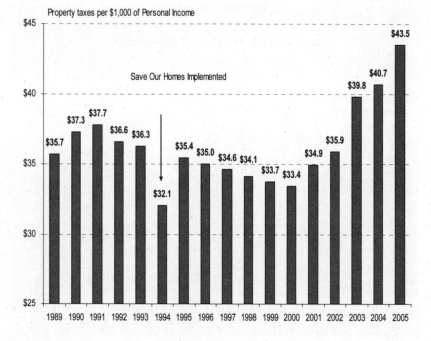

Property taxes per $1,000 of Personal Income

Save Our Homes Implemented

1989–2005[1]

---

[1] The 1994 property tax data reported by the Department of Revenue excludes Broward County. Consequently, the drop in total property tax levied reported does not imply an actual decline in statewide property tax levies. The evidence indicates that these revenues may have actually increased overall in 1994. We proceed with this analysis using the data reported by the Department of Revenue.

> *"Businesses tend to be interested in building and expanding in states whose courts have a fair and just environment."*
> Sean McBride

Standardized Business Courts

Problem: Courts are inefficient and inconsistent in resolving business disputes.

The majority of Florida business disputes are litigated in Florida's circuit courts, which are responsible for hearing claims of over $15,000, all felony cases, and various other matters. Nearly all complex business litigation begins in a circuit court. The number of lawsuits filed in Florida's circuit courts is increasing in line with Florida's population and economic growth. In fiscal year 2003–2004, there were 859,452 filings in Florida's circuit courts, a 21 percent increase since fiscal year 1994–1995. Currently, nineteen of the twenty judicial circuits do not have a system to process business litigation in a quick and efficient manner.

Solution: Create a business court division of circuit court.

Florida will <u>establish a business specialty court, which will create a business-friendly legal environment, stimulate economic growth and business relocation, and ensure business owners are afforded a fair and speedy resolution to their complex litigation issues.</u> This court should be mirrored after the business court division of the Ninth Circuit in Orlando. Business specialty courts make the resolution of business disputes more efficient and predictable, thereby attracting more business to Florida. In 2005, over 13,000 business lawsuits were filed in Orange County. Before the Ninth Circuit created its business court division, such suits were scattered among civil court judges. The Ninth Circuit developed rules delineating the type of complex business litigation to be directed to the new business division, such as antitrust actions, complex contract disputes, intellectual property cases, unfair competition claims, and business franchise disputes. These complex cases account for approximately 20 percent of the business litigation in the circuit.

Business courts provide a number of advantages. First, they assign business cases to judges with particular interest and expertise in business litigation, which enhances the consistency and accuracy of decisions on business law issues. Second, they generally reduce the time and costs involved in lengthy litigation. Finally, court rules can be tailored to the particular needs of these cases.

States with business courts report they have successfully used the existence of a business court to persuade businesses to locate and/or remain in those states. Business courts also benefit the court system as a whole by removing the burden of large, commercial cases from the general circuit court docket. This simple change will reduce costs for both the court system and businesses.

> *"Equal access to capital, industry, and technology—these are the current steps in the civil rights movement."* Jesse Jackson

Economic Civil Rights for Communities

Problem: Poverty exists in Florida cities.

Over the past ten years, Florida has experienced a nationally unrivaled economic boom. Unfortunately, that prosperity has not trickled down to our poorest urban centers and rural counties. During the 1990s, Republicans in the U.S. House of Representatives, seeking an alternative to the failed 1960s-era anti-poverty orthodoxy, approved welfare reform measures that overhauled thirty years of government entitlement programs. Today, notwithstanding these anti-poverty measures, Miami is one of America's poorest cities—an unacceptable designation. A *Miami Herald* article based on U.S. Census Bureau data identified Miami as the nation's third poorest major city after Cleveland and Detroit. Additionally, the Department of Children and Families' most recent Annual Report on Homeless Conditions in Florida approximates that over 85,900 persons are homeless on any given day. Moreover, the report estimates that over 60 percent of Florida's homeless have been homeless more than once (33 percent have been homeless four times or more), and

35 percent have been homeless for over one year. Chronic homeless cases—those who live on and off the streets for years—are usually the most expensive and difficult for a city to manage. Additionally, many of the state's rural areas lack the infrastructure to help alleviate poverty.

Solution: Promote urban revitalization and rural economic development.

Fostering growth in these downtrodden regions requires a bold, dramatic, and innovative approach to economic development and urban revitalization. The Legislature should institute a pilot program that creates a tax-free zone in the most economically depressed areas of our state. Florida must resolve to break down the economic obstacles that exist in many urban centers today with the same vigilance and zeal used to assail racial and gender barriers over the past forty years.

IDEA 98

This program will relieve existing and new businesses, within delineated boundaries, of the state sales tax, as well as the sales tax on the purchase of goods and services required for conducting their businesses. Additionally, new enterprises will be relieved of state document taxes.

The program should eventually be expanded to include zones designated as critical areas of poverty by Florida International University's study of Florida's municipalities. This targeted government support for the poorest areas of the state will focus on well-defined, proven areas of poverty. This approach is designed to remove cumbersome bureaucratic mechanisms and infuse the process with the free-market and entrepreneurial principles upon which America's economic success has been built.

Florida should also establish Housing First as an alternative to the prevalent system of emergency shelter/transitional housing. Housing First provides affordable housing to the homeless in poverty-stricken areas and is funded by a public-private initiative through which investors and volunteers alike can pledge funds or donate their time to help improve their communities.

Through Housing First policies, cities can create a measurable system of accountability to track success in getting the homeless off the street and into treatment, job training, and stable lives. A number of cities have experienced quantifiable success with Housing First; Philadelphia has seen a 60 percent drop in homelessness in the five years since it adopted the program, while San Francisco reports a 26 percent decrease in homelessness during its two-year program. Furthermore, in Denver rates of hospitalization, imprisonment, and commitment to detox centers fell 60 percent among program participants.

Housing First programs are generally cost-effective. The program lowered the costs of traditional homeless services in Denver from $70 million to $13 million. Annual spending on Housing First participants' non-emergency medical care, housing, and counseling averages $14,385, while the average case of indigent emergency medical care costs $29,000.

According to the United States Interagency Council on Homelessness, ten cities or counties in Florida have committed to implementing ten-year plans to end homelessness. Florida should expand the number of homeless campaigns in the state and ensure that these efforts include significant Housing First programs. If the success of these programs around the country can be duplicated in Florida, in time we may be able to eliminate homelessness completely.

> *"All the forces in the world are not so powerful as an idea whose time has come."* Victor Hugo

National Idea Bank

Problem: There is a lack of civic involvement and no coordinated database of ideas.

Idearaisers solicited the suggestions of residents across the state of Florida. Everywhere we went, participants offered great ideas on almost every issue imaginable, with the same proposals frequently put forward in different locations. It quickly became clear that great ideas abound in Florida, but we lack a central location to collect these ideas or enhance previous ideas that have already been implemented.

Solution: Create an "Idea Bank" where ideas are submitted and successful ideas are chronicled.

Florida will <u>create a nationwide, web-based "Idea Bank" that documents programs and initiatives that have succeeded.</u> This will be a showcase to present great ideas from organizations across the nation, such as A.L.E.C., N.C.S.L., and the Association of Mayors, and to give citizens the opportunity for civic participation by submitting ideas and watching them come to fruition. Furthermore, the Idea Bank will publish an annual list of the top ideas it has received throughout the year.

100ideas has already shown that citizens are eager for civic involvement when given the opportunity. Creation of a national Idea Bank will give all Americans the same opportunity the residents of Florida have enjoyed for the past two years.

Acknowledgments

Thousands of individuals are responsible for the content of this book, and we have been overwhelmed by the outpouring of ideas from the citizens of Florida. We have compiled a list of contributors, drawing from over 150 idearaisers and thousands of ideas submitted to our website. With so many names it is impossible to list everyone, and we apologize to anyone who was mistakenly omitted. We did not attach specific names to individual ideas, as most ideas appearing here were submitted numerous times in various forms, with the final versions reviewed by experts. We are continually grateful to every contributor.

Alessandro Abate
Drew Abel
Florence Aber
Chiquita Abney
Lourdes Abraham
Marta Abreu Telleria
Mercedes Acero
Samuel Acosta
Abdulia Acuna
Alex Adams
Brandon Adams
Greg Adams
Holly Adams
J. W. Adams
Alberto Adan
Douglas Adkins
Richard Agapay
Ray Agee
Suhaib Ahmad
Sameer Ahmed
Kimble Ainslie
Louis Alaimo
Antonio Alamo
Antonio Alavaro De Leon
Angel Alberto Alonso
Carlos Aldana
Linda Aldridge
Raquel Aleman
Michael Alexander
Tramell Alexander
Lidia Alfonse
Gustavo Alfonso

Amar Ali
Maria Alina Vinardell
Joan Allen
Larry Allen
Phillip Allen
Michael Allen
Nolan Allen
Robert Allen
Charles Aller
Luis Aller
Heather Allman
Gilberto Almeyda
Karen Almond
Eduardo Alonso
Roy Alonso
Karl Altenburger
Anibal Alvafrez
Celestino Alvarez
Cesar Alvarez
Consuelo Alvarez
Eladio Alvarez
Rina Alvarez
Nilo Alvarez
Sonnia Alvarodiaz
Angela Aly
Ilda Amor
Jim Anaston-Karas
Kim Anaston-Karas
Ronald Andersen
Mike Anderson
Mischelle Anderson
Noma Anderson

Robert Anderson
Vaughn Anderson
William Anderson
Pedro Andollo
Karen Andre
Luis Andreaci
Leandro Angel Oliva
Alex Annunziato
Mike Antczak
Al Anthony
Allison Anthony
Richard Antolinez
Vivian Ines Aquino-Sosa
Delia Aragon
Fabio Arber
Jose Arbide
Emperatriz Arias
Roberto Aristondo
Herbert Arkin
Jorge Armas
William Armellini
Jeff Arnold
Linda Arnold
Neil Arnott
Lisa Aronson
Leonel Arrazola
Catherine Arthur
Peter Arts
Paul Asfour
Clarence Ashcraft
Brad Ashwell
Maria Astrain
Rita Asuncion Calvo
Terry Atchley
Ron Audette
Walt Augustinowicz
Carlos Auino
Alison Austin
Marjorie Avery
Julio Avica
Terry Axelrod
Anthony Ayala
David Ayala
James Ayres
John Bachman
Ronald Bachman
Jude Bagatti
Jose Bahamondes
Robert Bailey
Ruth Bailey
Rob Bains
Andrew Baird
Luis Baires
Mike Bakboni
Glenn Baker
Dale Balke

Cheri Ball
Sandy Ballas
Blanco Balseiro
Rafael Baltazar
Maria Baluja
Ryan Banfill
Matthew Banker
Emelia Banos
John Baranzano
Leah Barber-Heinz
Edward Barberio
Thomas Barcus, Jr.
Harold Barley
Peter Barna
Ann Barnes
Candace Barnes
David Barnes
Harold Barnes
Jeff Barnes
Miriam Barnes
Ernie Barnett
Hunter Barnett
Tom Barnette
Ramon Barquin,III
Madeline Barredo
Lorenzo Barrenechea
JoAnn Barrett
Alex Barry
Dianne Barter
Thomas Barter
Doris Bartlett
Peter Bartolotti
Luis Basagoitia
Carole Baskin
Jennifer Bass
Lisa Bass
William Bassett
Ramiro Basto
Maria Basualdo
Karin Batchelder
Aldo Batista
Arthur Baum
Thomas Baumgartner
Melissa Baxley
Virginia Bayer
Beverly Beanland
Dick Beard
Nikki Beare
Abigail Beauchamp
Ofelia Becarril
Jorgelino Becerril
Abraham Bechily
Hayley Beck
Mayra Beers
Betsy Begens
Paul Belcher

Chris Belena
Kenton Bell
Howard Bell
Angela Bell-Deems
Raquel Bello
Delores Bellon
Vanessa Benavides
Juan Benguria
Alberto Benitez
Clara Benitez
Consuelo Benitez
Maria Benitez
Bill Bennington
Mark Benson
Rick Berg
Maria Bermudez
Kenneth Berns
Seymour Bernstein
Peter Berry
Rue Berryman
Wayne Bertsch
Daniel Bevarly
Laura Bhandari
Richard Biagi
Brett Bibeau
Brian Bickett
Jose Bilbao
Ron Bilbao
Hal Billerbeck
Marbeth Bingman
Lewis Binswanger
Stephen Birtman
Shelby Bishop
Michael Bittman
John Biver
Ronald Black
Rena Blades
Samuel Blair
Jeff Blake
Ashley Blakely
Katie Blalock
Patrick Blanc
Jane Blanchard
Lisa Blanchard
Manuel Blanco
Maria Blanco
Anne Blankenship
Mary Blankenship
Donnie Blanton
Mike Blevins
Pamela Blevins
Jeannette Bliss
Michael Blowers
Aaron Blum
Charles Blythe
Sandra Boccuzzo

Morris Bodoia
Alex Bohler
Bonnie Boisvert
Willy Bolivar
Joshua Bomstein
Reinaldo Bonachea
Joanna Bonfanti
Jay Bonham
Andy Bontempo
Carolyn Booth
Tracey Booth
Colin Boothby
Darvin Boothe
Mike Borns
Augusto Borras
Ena Borras
Mireyes Borras
Roberto Borroto
Kim Bosket
Clarence Bostic
Ethan Boston
Bonnie Bostrom
Christine Botticol
Carolyn Boudreau
Joe Bourassa
Dale Bourdette
Jack Bovee
Allen Bowles
Ron Bowman
Lesley Boyd
Markisha Boykin
Scott Boylan
Julio Bracho
William Bracken
Kenneth Bradley
Margie Bradley
Markeeta Brady
Teresa Brady
Peggy Bramka
Sean Brandow
Daniel Brannen
James Branno
Bill Brasfield
Evelyn Braun
Ernesto Bravo
Maria Bravo
Mercedes Bravo
Karen Breakell
Edward Breslin
Don Bressler
Clayton Brett
Tina Brewer
Alfonso Brewster
David Brickhouse
Jess Bridenstine
Phyllis Bridges

Timothy Brightbill
Jose Bringuez
Juan Brito
Orlando Brito
Julie Britton
Jeanette Brock
John Brockman
Sarah Brody
Bob Brogna
Mary Bronough
Clifford Brooks
George Brooks
Maj. John Brooks
Heather Brosi
Brandi Brown
Janice Brown
Judith Brown
Karen Brown
Keith Brown
Larry Brown
Michael Brown
Rana Brown
Rebecca Brown
Robert Brown
Steven Brown
Terry Brown
Toni Brown
Sharon Brownfield
B. Brubaker
Robert Bruce
Mary Lou Brunell
Peggy Bruner
Rene Brunet
J. Brustad
Andrea Bryan
Jane Bryan
Dave Bryant
Karen Bryant
Kyle Bucher
Douglas Buck
Robert Buckholz
John Buckley
Bill Buffington
Manuel Buigas
David Bundy
Kirill Bune
Vivian Burch
Herlin Burch
Frank Burgess
Joan Burke
Frederick Burman
Pamela Burnette
Gaye Burnham
Susan Burns
Bonnie Burnsaw
Lance Burri

Joy Busby
Gregory Busch
Karen Bush
Shuan Butcher
Robert Butler
Richard Button
Rosie Byrd
Lelis Caballos
Bill Cabana
Carlos Cabanas
Marta Cabanas
Jose Miguel Cabanas
Margareta Cabezas
Pedro Cabezas
Victor Cabral
Francisco Cabrera
Luis Cabrera
Hilda Cadenas
Joie Cadle
Welton Cadwell
Ron Cahen
Christa Calamas
Jose Calero
Gloria Calhoun
Marion Callahan
Jared Callan
Doug Callaway
Genara Calmet
Catalina Calvo
David Calvo
Yolanda Calzado
Scott Cambles
Luis Cameio
Elizabeth Campbell
Harvey Campbell
Ana Campos
William Cance
Saul Candido Reyes
Chris Canino
Robert Cannon
Roy Cannon
Jose Canosa
Gloria Cantens Gomez
Mireya Capdevila
Yolanda Capo
C. Capote
Marianne Capoziello
Lilia Caraballo
Isaac Carballo
Rita Carballo
David Carbone
J. Carbonell
Jorge Carbonell
Eduardo Carbonell
Dan Cardona
Art Carlson

Kelly Carlson
Elsa Carmen Leon
Olga Carnet
Adam Carnow
Patricia Carpio
Marsan Carr
Antonia Carrasco
Martha Carrasco
Carmen Carratala
Gabriel Jose Carrera
Thomas Carrero
Gary Carriere
Juan Carrocera
Charles Carroll
Chuck Carter
Judy Carter
Joe Caruncho
Linda Caruso
Lazaro Casamayor
Michael Cassara
Gisela Castellanos
Maria Luisa Castellanos
Alexander Castillo
Timothy Castle
Gabriel Castro
Bert Castro
Divaldo Castro
Nick Castro
Silvia Castro
Alberto Castro Gomez
Jose Castro-Toirac
Jim Catron
Michele Causey
M. Cavanaugh
Jorge Cedeno
Leonel Cedeno
Rudy Cegielski
Saul Celin
Jorge Cendan
Belen Cervantes
Inci Ceurvels
Jorge Chabebe
Jane Chambeaux
Thomas Chamberlain
Jonathan Chambers
Giselle Chamizo
Elizabeth Chandler
Juan Chao
Linda Chapin
DA Chapman
James Chastain
Sue Chavers
Jodi Chemes
Eric Cherry
Shannon Chesser
Eva Chester

Amelia Chirole
Deloris Chome-Herschoff
Lawrence Chrietzberg
Ty Christian
Carla Christianson
Ladd Christina
Margaret Chubb
Maria Ciervide Valdes
Dominick Cirotti
Susan Cirotti
Joan Claridge
Angel Clark
Don Clark
Tonya Clark
Patricia Clarke
Steven Claus
Judith Clayton
Peter Cleary
Noel Cleland
Jean Clements
Robert Clements
Eve Cline
Don Cloud
Melissa Coakley
Dianne Cobb
Katherine Cobleigh
Kent Cockson
Barbara Coffee
Christopher Cogle
Irv Cohen
Marc Cohen
Sam Cohen
Barbara Cohen Pippin
Donald Coleman
Karen Cole-Smith
Franklin Coley
Thomas Colgan
Alec Colley
Guido Colli
Fernando Colli
Chris Collins
John Collins
Linda Collins
Michael Collins
Tony Collins
Erin Collinsworth
Angel Colls
Angelina Colonneso
Gary Comfort
Tim Common
Suellen Cone
Richard Conklin
L. Conlon
Gordon Connell
Thomas Connell
Kathleen Connors

Robert Connors
Amanda Conochalla
Kyle Considder
Cathy Consolo
Gail Cook
Carolyn Cooke
Vicki Cooley
Connie Cooper
Roger Cooper
Samuel Cooper
Susan Copening
Blair Corbett
Finlay Corbin
Noreen Corcoran
Ted Corcoran
Gail Cordial
William Cordle
Alina Corsa Campos
Delia Cortada
Robert Corti
Carlos Cortina
Fred Cosby
Stephen Cosgrove
Janice Costa
Rocco Costello
Oliver Costich
Christine Cothron
Kathleen Cotier
Ralph Cotier
Deborah Courtney
Martha Couto
John Cox
Linda Cox
Robert Cox
Melissa Coyle
Dan Crago
Rita Craig
Catherine Craig-Myers
Fredric Cramer
Nancy Craney
Jim Crawford
Toni Creamer
Dawn Credle
Jean Creek
Eugenio Crespo
Miriam Crespo
Steffan Cress
Peter Crisanti
Candice Critchfield
Philip Crowder
Thomas Crumlish
Bill Cruz
Edel Cruz
Preciliano Cruz
John Cserep
Gayle Cubberley

Douglas Cueny
Lissette Cuervo
David Culp
Ernest Culp
Katie Cundy
John Cunningham
Anthony Cutaia
Becky Cwiek
Steven Czonstka
Steve Dackson
Robert Dahlen
John Dailey
William Dalton
Bobbie Damp
Michael Danchuk
Bob Danforth
David Daniel
Derick Daniel
Lilia Daniel
Kenneth Daniels
Linda Daniels
Sheryl Daniels
Kim Darin
Art Darling
Lynn Darrell
D. Daugherty
William David
Ann Davis
Gene Davis
Janette Davis
Janie Davis
John Davis
Kevan Davis
Bill Davison
Joe Davison
Brandi Day
F. de Cossio
Luis De Hernandez
Delia de la Pena
Jose de la Pena
Rebecca De la Rosa
Jose de la Vega
Vickie de Oro
Jose De Pablo
Christopher De Ture
Carlos De Varona
Margarita De Varona
Richard de Villiers
Roberto De Zayas Garcia
Amy Dean
Claudia Dean
Elisa Dean
Gesell Dean
Roger Dearing
Charles DeArmond
Dwight DeBoer

Reid Decker
Cheryl DeCou
David Deehl
Paul DeGiusti
Michael Deichen
David Del Gallo
Nidia Del Socoro Priede
Norie del Valle
Terry Delahunty
Bruce DeLaney
Marie Delaney
Ines Deleon
Julio Delgado
Luis Delgado
Martha Delgado
Fred DeLoach
Paul deMange
Diane DeMark
JoAnn DeMine
David Demond
Michelle Dennard
Michael Dennehy
Lucinda Deputy
Mike Deren
Curt Deslatte
Alice Detore
Susana Deutsch
Dave Dewis
John Dewitt
Antonio Diaz
Carlos Diaz
Felix Diaz
Jesus Diaz
Jose Diaz
Juana Diaz
Margarita Diaz
Maria Diaz
Norma Diaz
Rachel Diaz
Raul Diaz
Roberto Diaz
Frank DiBello
William Dick
Allen Dickinson
Rita Dickinson
Julia Dieguez
Paul Diehl
Marisol Diestro
Robert Digby
George Diller
Esta Dilley
Bradford Dillman
William Dillon
John Dimbat
Joseph Dinerman
Maggie Dipietra

Tony Disarcina
Angela Ditmore
Walter Dix
Christina Dixon
David Dixon
Lisa Dixon
Thomas Dixon
Evan Dobkin
Quintin Docampo
Andrea Dockery
Derek Dodd
Consuelo Dodge
Ralph Dodge
Wendy Dodge
Henry Doenlen
George Dombrowski
Evelio Dominguez
Maria Don
Claire Donaghue
Sergio Donikian
Bob Donley
Jeff Donnelly
Kevin Donnelly
Michael Dooley
Olga Doran
PJ Dotson
David Douglas
D. Doyle
Ron Draa
Noel Duarte
Anne Dufault
Paul Duncan
Sandy Dunfee
Deborah Dunman
Charles Dunn
William Dunn
Delsa Duran
Elina Duran
Joe Durek
M. Dwyer
Erick Dyke
Katherine Dyko
Christopher Earl
Michael Earley
Mary Ellen Early
Mack Eason
Steve Ecenia
Berto Echevarria
Belva Eddins
Julie Eddy
Jan Edeburn
John Edge
John Edwards
Pete Edwards
Tom Edwards
Donald Eiler

Iris Eisenberg
Ginger Eisenrod
Eric Eisnaugle
Ronald Eldridge
Teodoro Eleverria
Phil Elliott
Roger Elliott
Clyde Ellis
Kim Emerson
Bee Epley
Ulf Erlingsson
H. Erskine
John Ervin
Joan Erwin
Gustavo Escalona
Ruth Esper
Laura Esslinger
Enrique Estavillo
Rick Estavillo
Rachwal Esther
Nicolle Etchart
Irene Euchler
Catherine Evanoff
Judith Evans
Gail Evans
Rodney Everhart
Phil Everingham
Edna Mae Everitt
Flora Evon
Ray Evon
Manuel Extramil
Olivia Fabre
James Failor
Elizabeth Fairweather
Armando Fana
Jim Fannin
John Fanning
Janet Fansler
K. Fanti
Horacio Farina
Anita Farley
Joe Farley
Adam Farmer
Allison Farr
Rachael Fasciani
Phillip Faulk
John Fawell
Shawn Fedigan
Barbara Feeney
Carmen Feijoo
Travis Felder
Margarita Feliz
Stephen Fell
Steve Fell
Amelia Fernandez
Ana Fernandez

Elia Fernandez
Gonzalo Fernandez
Manny Fernandez
Maria Fernandez
Mirtha Fernandez
Ofelia Fernandez
Roberto Fernandez
Maria Fernandez Stinson
Beatriz Ferreiro
Charlie Fetscher
Nicole Fey
Josefina Figueredo
Perfecto Figueroa
Robert Fine
Paul Finelli
Paul Finelli
Scott Finkel
Debra Finnel
Aidan Finnerty
David Fischer
Camille Fisher
N. Fisher
Ralph Fisher
Howard Fisher
Ed FitzGerald
Patricia Fitzgerald
Jennifer Fitzwater
Bob Flaige
William Flake
Erica Flanders
Richardo Fleitas
Juan Fleites
Kathy Flemming
James Fletcher
David Florance
Javier Flores
Juan Flores
Maria Flores
Marie Flores
Loretta Flowers
Pat Flynn
Bruce Fogarty
James Fogarty
Wayne Fogel
Amy Foley
Erin Foley
Karen Foley
Onelia Fonseca
Candido Font
Mark Fontaine
Carlton Forbes
Bob Ford
Ginny Foreman
Debrah Forester
Ken Forrester
Jane Foster

Learn more about Regnery books!

Dear Reader,

Thank you for buying this Regnery book. To learn more about Regnery Publishing, as well as upcoming and existing books, please fill out this postcard and drop it in the mail.

Thank you,

Marji Ross
President and Publisher

Enter your email here: _____

Name _____

Address _____

City _____ State _____ Zip _____

CHPT-B

Shelley Foster
Ron Fournier
Mary Ellen Fowler
Crispin Fowler
Leon Fowler
Eduardo Fraga
Francisco Framil
Maureen France
Rene Francis
Charles Francis
Joy Frank
Morton Frankel
Joe Frasca
Sivan Fraser
Stephanie Frazier
Russell Frederick
Cara Freedman
Mark Freedman
Mitch Freedman
R. Dale French
Judson French
Antonio Frexes
Arturo Freyre
Manuel Freyre
Maria Freyre
Dennis Freytes
Gladys Frias
Jorge Frias
Gertrude Friedman
Douglas Friend
Emily Friend
George Fritschi
George Fritschi
Reggie Frye
Carol Fuchs
Sherry Fudim
Hilda Fuentes
Jesus Fuentes
Vincent Fulton
Bruce Furino
Jack Furnari
Jack Furney
Pedro Fuster
May Fuze
Pat Gadban
Gayle Gaines
Jerry Gallagher
Raquel Gallegos
Carl Galloway
Darlyn Galloway
William Gandy
Croitiene GanMoryn
Richard Garber
Amanda Garces
Hortensia Garces
Nibardo Garces

Rafael Garcia
Roman Garcia
Alina Garcia
Dolores Garcia
Elda Garcia
Emilia Garcia
Evanisto Garcia
Gabino Garcia
Humberto Garcia
Ledia Garcia
Manuel Garcia
Maria Garcia
Miguel Garcia
Modesto Garcia
Peter Garcia
Ray Garcia
Reggie Garcia
Rosa Garcia
Urielle Garcia
Raul Garcia
Guillermo Garcia Alvarez
Eula Gardner
Mike Gardner
Joseph Gariboldi
Eric Garner
Kathy Garten
Alberto Gasti
Dayna Gaut
Christie Gauthier
Bryant Gay
Douglas Gaynor
George Geisler
George Geletko
Paulette Geller
Judy Genshaft
Paul Gentsch
Shirley Gerstenberger
Amanda Ghaffari
Helen Ghanem
Patricia Giantomenico
Francis Gibbons
Mark Gibson
Juan Gil
Judy Gilick
Carolyn Gill
Hank Gill
Tom Gill
Kathy Gilland
David Gilley
Ray Gilley
Tony Gilman
Don Gilmore
Suzann Gilmore
Sharon Gilstrap
Joel Gingery
Barb Gingham

Catherine Giordano
Rick Giordano
Frank Girodano
James Glass
J. Carey Gleason
Raymond Glessner
Marta Gobel
Greg Goebel
Kim Goebert
Marion Goh
Alberta Gold
Gary Goldberg
William Goldberg
Randy Golden
Lawrence Goldman
Richard Goldman
Carole Goldsmith
Jason Goldtrap
Hilda Gomez
Humberto Gomez
Isabel Gomez
Jaime Gomez
Jorge Gomez
Luis Gomez
Tim Gomez
Estela Gomez
Jose Gomez-Bustillo
Paulina Gomez-Bustillo
Aleida Gonzalez
Angela Gonzalez
Aurora Gonzalez
Blanca Gonzalez
Enrique Gonzalez
Eugenio Gonzalez
George Gonzalez
Hilda Gonzalez
Isabel Gonzalez
Jean Gonzalez
Jesus Gonzalez
José Gonzalez
Josefina Gonzalez
Juan Gonzalez
Larry Gonzalez
Louis Gonzalez
Manuel Gonzalez
Maria Gonzalez
Mario Gonzalez
Miguel Gonzalez
Miretta Gonzalez
Pedro Gonzalez
Rob Gonzalez
Rodolfo Gonzalez
Rolando Gonzalez
Sara Gonzalez
Elisha Gonzalez-Bonnewitz
James Good

Laura Goodhue
Frank Goodin
Carey Goodman
Debby Goodman
Nina Goodrich
Ann Gordon
Charles Gordon
Rick Gordon
Seth Gordon
Suzanne Gordon
Janet Goree
Lesbet Gorges
Jan Gorrie
Michael Gorsetman
George Govin
Dave Gowan
Provi Grafals
Marilyn Graham
Tim Gramling
Gisela Granado
Magda Granda
Fred Grant
Diana Grawitch
Sean Grebey
Don Grecko
Troy Grecko
Clayton Green
Kathy Green
Phillip Green
Charlotte Greenbarg
Harold Greenberg
Barbara Greene
Judith Greene
William Greeves
Andrea Gregg
Ryan Gregg
Nicole Greggs
Frank Gregoire
Sheila Griffin
Crystal Griffith
IC Griffith
Cheryl Griffiths
Daniel Grillone
Barbara Gross
Marla Gross
Paul Gross
William Gross
Nicki Grossman
Richard Grzych
Ramon Guell
Karl Guenther
Robert Guerin
Lila Guerra
Luis Guerra
Reynaldo Guerra
Hector Guevara

Julia Guia
Roberto Guia
Norm Gulkis
Lee Gullett
Sheldon Gusky
Lidia Gutierrez
Manuela Gutierrez
Margarita Gutierrez
Jose Gutierrez-Ruz
Gloria Guzman
Robert Haas
Mel Haber
Scott Hackmyer
Arlene Hadley
Ted Haeussner
Linda Hagedorn
Jill Hagen
Brendan Haggerty
Joyce Haggerty
Briana Hagquist
Michael Haines
Lester Hairs
Norma Hairston
Rebecca Hait
Colin Halbach
Charles Hall
Andrew Hall
Bill Hall
David Hall
John Hall
Lisa Hall
Natalie Hall
Marilynn Hallman
Craig Ham
Mark Hamilton
Jennifer Hancock
Todd Hand
Richard Hannon
Wendy Hansen
Catherine Hanson
Jeanine Hanson
John Happy
Gilda Harden
William Harden
Lori Harding
Richard Harding
Dan Hare
Sally Harkness
Steve Harness
James Harrell
Camille Harris
John Harris
Richard Harris
Theodis Harris
Debra Harrison
Frank Harrison

Ivette Harrouche
Lynn Harrow
Betty Harstad
Ollie Harter
Diana Hartman
Jean Hartman
Bob Hartnett
Gary Hartzler
Elissa Harvey
Lori Harvey
Glenn Hastings
Woodrow Hatcher
Mike Hathaway
Bruce Hauptli
Bruce Hausman
Ed Havill
Eliza Hawkins
Dee Hawks
Chester Hawthorne
Doug Haynam
Christopher Haynes
John Haynie III
Tarry Hays
Ann Heaton
David Hebert
Erik Hector
Patrick Heffernan
Chiquita Henderson
Donna Henderson
Joel Henderson
Robert Hendry
Juan Henley
Dan Henry
Mary Hensel
Kenneth Hensley
David Herbster
Frank Herhold
Fred Hering
Karen Heriot
Eulogio Hermida
Donna Hernandez
Eduardo Hernandez
Helena Hernandez
Homobono Hernandez
Jose Hernandez
Margarita Hernandez
Mercedes Hernandez
Jose Manuel Hernandez
Filiberto Herrera
Jose Herrera
Laura Herrera
Lois Herron
Robert Herron
Zachary Hersman
Attila Hevesy
Allison Heyden

Richard Hickok
Carol Hicks
Gary Hicks
Bill Higgins
Melanie Higgins
Donald Hill
Jeremy Hill
Joann Hill
Mike Hill
Robert Hill
Susana Hillman
Jason Hindle
Terri Hinds
Brian Hinton
Dean Hinton
Maeva Hipps
Kenneth Hirsch
Shirley Hirsch
William Histed
John Hitt
Tra Hitt
Donna Hodges
Jacob Hoechst
Kevin Hoeft
Ronald Hoelzer
Mercedes Hoffmann
Peter Hofstra
Vidya Hogan
Stephen Hogge
Billy Holcombe
Christopher Holland
Gary Holland
Steven Holland
Robbie Hollenbeck
Barbara Hollinger
Darrin Holloman
Wallace Holmes
Dan Holsenbeck
Bryon Holz
Susanne Homant
Ruby Homayssi
Venita Hood
Jackie Hopercraft
Craig Hopes
Scott Hopes
Lane Hoppen
Ann Horgas
Claire Hornstein
Rogelio Horta
Malinda Horton
Marsha Hosack
Garrett Hoskins
Rosanne Howard
Scott Howat
James Howell
Karen Howell

Linda Howell
Patrick Howell
Valerie Howell
Paul Howland
Edwin Hubbard
Keith Hubbard
Patricia Huff
David Hughes
Sharon Hughes
Marta Hugue
Elias Huguet
Dale Humphrey
Stephen Humphrey
Joseph Humphreys
Joe Humphries
Patricia Humphries
Joni Hunt
Barbara Hunter
Rene Hurtado
Julie Hutchingson
Steph Hyatt
George Ibarra
Elsa Ibarra
Sue Idtensohn
Carlos Iglesias
Ezequiel Infante
Charlene Inglis
Juan Isaza
Belinda Itson
Dwayne Ivory
Jessi Izhakoff
Cyndy Jackman
Michael Jacks
Brenda Jackson
Rita Jackson
Diane Jacob
Mickey Jacob
Walt Jacobi
Donna Jacobi Pruett
Anna Jacobs
Steve Jacoby
Michelle Jacquis
Barbara Jaehne
Patricia James
Manuela Janak
Jesus Jara
Clara Jaramillo
Maria Jaramillo
Sami Jarrah
Carole Jean Jordan
Robert Jeanguenat
Susan Jeanguenat
William Jefferson
Michele Jenkins
Kim Jernigan
Paul Jess

Nate Jessup
Michael Jimenez
Miguel Jimenez
Aisha Johnson
Gary Johnson
Kelly Johnson
Kenneth Johnson
Lee Johnson
Sonya Johnson
Tilicia Johnson
Jane Johnston
Tara Johnston
Ruth Jones
Camille Jones
Darrel Jones
Dug Jones
Jimmy Jones
Kinzy Jones
Larry Jones
Leroy Jones
Mack Jones
Maryellen Jones
Ron Jones
Ryan Jones
Susan Jones
Tom Jones
Vernon Jones
Stephen Joost
Barbara Jordan
Delores Jordan
Saba Jote
Esther Jove
Michael Joyce
Mike Joynes
Susan Juan
Sallye Jude
Georgina Julian
Joe Justice
Jack Kader
Cory Kalifch
Donna Kalil
Abraham Kamarck
Kay Kammel
David Kapaun
Hurant Karibian
Robert Karns
Steven Kasdin
Karen Kateley
Alex Katsaros
Charlotte Kay
Christopher Kearney
Alan Keck
Art Keeble
William Kegan
Arthur Keiser
Robert Keith

Kitt Kelleher
Walter Keller
Dorothy Kelley
Laura Kelley
Juan Kelly
Jason Kendall
Roger Kenneally
Duncan Kennedy
Eric Kennedy
Josephine Kennell
Jennifer Keskinen
Charlotte Kesten
Kelly Keyes
Renu Khator
Thomas Kibler
Cecil Kidd
Shirley Kilkelly
Edward Killeen
Jonathan Kilman
Renee Kilroy
Bonnie King
Marti King
Susan King
Tiffany King
Katrina Kinnard-Rini
Marcelle Kinney
Arthur Kirk
Maggie Kirkpatrick
Becky Kirsch
Jesse Kirsch
Brenda Kitch
Mike Klapka
Shelley Klausman
Heatherjoy Klein
Mary Klein
Twila Klein
Linda Kleindienst
Levko Klos
Joan Knerr
Margot Knight
Rick Knight
Trish Knobel
Fred Kohly
Jeffrey Koletsky
Lawrence Kolin
Jennie Konopasek
Carol Koogler
Delores Koontz
Dan Kosoff
Charles Kossuth
Patricia Kraft
Dan Krassner
Cheryl Krause
Gail Kreib
Gertrud Kuckhahn
Karen Kuether

Donald Kurney III
Dale Kurzejewski
Brett Kushner
Michael Kutell
Wayne La Mura
Lindsey LaBate
Rich LaBelle
Renee LaBerge
Patricia LaBrot
N. Laca
Dean Lafrentz
Don Laird
Gloria Lamar
Brian Lamb
Cynthia Lambert
George Lambka
Rosemarie Lamm
Donna Lance
Sharon Land Rousey
John Landon
John Lane
Brad Langdon
Ernest Langdon
Becky Lannon
Mariann Lansing
Berta Lapez
Maria Lapiz
William Large
Diane LaRochelle
Daniel Larrison
Melody Larson
Xiomara Larzabal
John Lasek
Denise Lasher
Martha Lasseter
Ted Latour
Isabel Lau
Louis Laubscher
Carol Lauer
Joelle Lau-Hansen
Marta Laura
Dixto Lavandero
Cira Lavandero
Tracey Lavoll
Doralee Law
Phil Lawanson
Kristina Lawrence
Jerry Lawson
Barbara Leach
Stephen Leatherman
Renne Leatto
Victor Leavengood
Jerry Lechliter
Emo Ledestich
Alexander Lee
David Lee

Don Lee
Scott Leeseberg
Ann Leffard
Marti Leib
RE LeMon
Renee Lemonier
Carole Lennis
Ana Leon
Jean Lepley
Barbara Leslie
Steve Leute
Linda Levin
Morton Levine
Evemarie Lewin
Ella Lewis
Gloria Lewis
Rene Lewis
Thomas Lewis
Jay Lewitt
James Ley
William Leyda
Ada Libertad Barilari
Howard Libin
Elaine Liftin
Johnny Limbaugh
Amanda Linares
Martin Linares
Virginia Lind
Viviane Lindeolsson
Vickie Lindsey
Meredith Linley
Susan Litchfield
Donna Litowitz
Cindy Littlejohn
Lazara Llauro
Richard Lockhart
Robin Loebel
Deborah London
Sherron Long
Todd Long
Calvin Longacre
Kristen Longmore
Earle Loomis
Paul Looney
Jorge Lopez
Amandalina Lopez
Camita Lopez
Christina Lopez
Francisco Lopez
Georgina Lopez
Larry Lopez
Luis Lopez
Ricardo Lopez
Carlos Lopez-Chavez
Orlando Lorenzo
Julia Lotito

Steven Lott
Tod Lotz
Jessica Lowe
Terri Lowery
William Lowery
Dan Lucas
DM Lucas
Sheri Lucas
Ned Luczynski
Thomas Lunsford
Mark Lust
Laura Lutz
Norman Lynn
Patti Lynn
Jason Lynne
Ann Lyons
Michael Lyons
Lake Lytal Jr.
Stewart Lytle
Janet Mabry
Bill MacDonald
Michelle MacDonald
Karen MacFarland
J. Bernard Machen
Maria Macias
Alex Macintyre
Theodore Mack
Diane Mackie
James MacMahan
Hugh MacMillan
Steve MacMillan
Catherine Maddox
Alberto Madrigal
Marian Mager
Modesto Maidique
Wayne Malaney
Edward Malcer
Mary Frances Mancuso
Dorothy Mann
Ed Mann
Shana Manning
Tom Manning
Alfredo Manrarra
Douglas Mansell
Roberto Marante
John Marble
Sara Marc
Frank Marcani
Marcos Marchena
Benjamin Marcus
Maria Elena Margolles
Lisa Margulis
Andrew Marinello
Danielle Marino
Carlos Maristany
Mirian Maristany

Bill Markin
Anne Marks
Jose Marquez
Danilo Marrero
Domingo Marriero
Jaqueline Marsach
Floyd Marsh
Hill Marsha
Paulette Marshall
Suzanne Marshall
Jose Martel
Pastora Marti
Frank Martin
Henree Martin
Jeremy Martin
Nelson Martin
Timothy Martin
Jose Martinez
Aida Martinez
Bertha Martinez
Christina Martinez
Luis Martinez
Mario Martinez
Miguel Martinez
Roberto Martinez
Teresa Martinez
Ann Masala
Guillermo Mascaro
James Mascola
Daniel Mason
Steve Mason
Melody Masuda
Alfonso Mateo
John Matheny
Charlotte Mather
Marcia Mathes
Peggy Mathews
Gene Matthews
Raymond Matthews
Cara Mattingly
Sandra Mattos
Jason Maxwell
Melanie May
Todd May
Digma Maya
Robert Mayberry
Doug Mayer
Margery Mayer
Darlene Maynard
Gabriel Mayor
Rebecca Mazzarella
Jimmie McAdams
John McArthur
Dolores McBride
John McBride
Lawrence McCabe

John McCaffrey
James McCalister
Doug McCarthy
Jess McCarty
Kathleen McCarty
Larry McCarty
Philip McCleary
Jim McClellan
Dean McCloud
Robert McClure
Georgia McCrary
Steve McCrea
Dana McCrone
Phil McDaniel
Chuck McDearmont
Mac McDonald
Jim McDowell
Neal McGarry
Kevin McGavin
Glenda McGee
Darrick McGhee
Matt McGill
John McGruder
Suzanne McGuire
Aleisa McGuirl
Bob McKee
Betty McKinley
Lara McKnight
Joseph McLain
George McLaughlin
Richard McLaurin
Terry McMahan
Joanne McMahon
Vicki McManus
Bonnie McMillan
Daniel McMurtrie
Trudy McNair
Catherine McNamara
Robert McNelis
Patric McPoland
Jack McRay
John McReynolds
Harry Mead
Edi Meadows
MaryEllen Meagher
Elsa Medina
David Meehan
Terry Meek
Carol Meeks
Wellington Meffert
Danese Mehaffey
Alexis Meizoso
Cynthia Melendez
Elsa Melendi
James Mellman
Marvin Melnick

Lydia Melville
Aida Menderos
Georgina Mendez
Guillermo Mendez
Gustavo Mendez
Arturo Menendez
Dinorah Menendez
Elsa Menendez
Gladys Menendez
Ramon Menendez
Dianne Mennitt
Mark Merrian
Elaine Merritt
Kathy Merritt
Bill Merwin
Julian Mesa
Lazaro Mesa
Harold Messerschmidt
Michael Mett
David Meyer
Ed Middleswart
Maria Mier
Lucia Mijares
Amber Mikluscak
Ocariz Milagros
Fred Miley
S. Milford
Connie Milito
Albert Miller
Bennett Miller
Brett Miller
Carmella Miller
Emil Miller
Melanie Miller
Paul Miller
Robert Miller
Sam Miller
Stephanie Miller
Terry Miller
Lora Lee Mills-Gregory
Bernice Milton
Albert Minger
Henry Minor
Isela Mirabal
Blanca Miranda
Rosemary Miranda
Salvador Miret
Jose Miro
Glenn Mitchell
Maria Mitchell
Maria Modesta Martinez
Thomas Moher
Bob Mohler
Elia Mollinedo
Lowell Momberg
Ivette Monaco

Kenneth Monaco
Carolyn Mondschein
Chris Monkaitis
Tiki Mont
Felix Montanez
Blanca Montejo
Braulia Montescieo
Robert Montgomery
David Moore
Jonathan Moore
Lennon Moore
Michele Moore
Richard Moore
Christine Moore Curtis
Emily Moorhouse
Alina Morales
Gisela Morales
Gloria Morales
Julia Morales
Marco Morales
Miriam Morales
Woody Morasco
Ivette Moreda
Charles Morel
Eduardo Moreno
Jenifer Moreno
Mercedes Moreno
Belita Moreton
Marita Morgado
Roberto Morgado
James Morgan
Linda Morgan
Alejandro Morin
Jim Morin
Paul Morline
Xio Maria Morrera
Kari Morris
Rich Morris
Diana Morrison
Richard Morrison
Rebecca Morrow
Joseph Mosca
James Mosher
Daniel Moslek
Leobardo Mota
Juan Manuel Moya
Teresa Moya
Fred Moyse
Tadar Muhammad
Jeffrey Muir
Lynn Mulherin
Stephen Mulkey
Patricia Mullay
Jim Mullen
Thomas Muller
Donald Mullins

Vickie-Jean Mullins
Wade Mullins
Anne Mullis
Jim Mumaw
Hortensia Muniz
Lourdes Munos
Eddy Munoz
Linda Munroe
Rick Munsell
Shirley Murphy
Tina Murphy
Brett Murray
Fran Murray
James Murray
Kathy Murray
Ned Murray
William Murry
Jim Murtha
Donna Murtzenard
Alice Myers
Margarett Myers
Patty Myers
Bruce Mylrea
Kelly Nagle
Russell Nansen
Cathy Nasby
Lee Nasehi
Edward Nasello
Andreas Navarro
Caridad Navarro
Carmen Navarro
Delia Navarro
Jesus Navarro
Paul Neidhart
Cheryl Nekola
Frank Nekola
Nancy Nelmes
Deborah Nelson
Doug Nelson
Gregory Nelson
Mark Nelson
Nancy Nelson
Robert Nelson
Mark Neppl
Marc Nerenstone
Wayne NeSmith
Dot Nettles
Carl Neu
Mary Neville
Elizabeth New
Margaret Newcomer
Norma Newman
Cory Newton
Barbara Nicholson
David Nicholson
John Nicks

Ryan Nicoletto
Rosemary Nieves
Cliff Nilson
Larry Nissen
Bruce Nissen
Frank (Bud) Nocera
Clara Noda
Beatriz Nora Gutierrez
Shelby Norris
Kelly Norton
Chris Norwood
Diana Nosti
Mireille Nosti
David Nottingham
Ricardo Nouel
Juan Nunez
John Nydegger
Don Nyman
Donald Nyman
Thomas O'Brien
Mark O'Bryant
Anne O'Bannon
Charles Obergfoll
Janice Oberwetter
Trudy O'Brien
Bobbie O'Brien
Noel Ocariz
Mike O'Connell
Patricia O'Connell
Adam O'Connor
George Oertel
Cheryl Oestreich
John Oestreich
Sandy Oestreich
Donald Ogden
Marshall Ogletree
James O'Hara
Dana O'Hara Smith
Arthur Olafsen
Ken O'Leary
Alice Olejnik
Carie Olivieri
Sheila Olsen
Jon Olson
Mollie O'Neill
Jeffrey Orenstein
Tracy O'Rourke
Pete Orsi
Caridad Ortega
Belinda Ortiz
Lance Ortiz
Mayte Ortiz
Shelia Osann
Robert Osik
Neil Oslos
Maria Gabriela Pacheco

Dawn Pack
Pedro Padres
Pedro Padron
Andre Paez
Eylin Pages
Gloria Palacios
Skydria Palma
Tom Palmer
Tiofilo Panchero
Nicholas Panos
Bessy Pantaja
Ted Pappas
Lucinda Pappert
Maria Paradelo
Chuck Pardee
Francisco Pardo
Trey Paris
Ava Parker
Dave Parker
David Parker
Gary Parker
Seana Parker-Dalton
Richard Parks
Isabel (Izzy) Parrado
Fred Parrulli
Josefina Pascua
Bev Passerello
John Passerello
Raimundo Pastor
Betty Paterson
Beach Patricia
Jim Patrick
Mike Patrone
Michael Patterson
Marylou Patton
Hilda Paula
Carleen Paule
Gunnar Paulson
Bob Payne
Don Payton
Kenneth Peach
Ona Pedreira
Nancy Peek McGowan
Steven Peisach
Mark Pelesh
Victorino Pena
Larry Pendarvis
Ofelia Penichet
Arthur Penney
Robert Peraza
Earl Perdue
Carlos Perea
Pedro Perez
Alicia Perez
Raul Perez
Sabino Perez

Carlos Perez
Eduardo Perez
Edwin Perez
Louis Perez
Matilde Perez
Pablo Perez
Rogelia Perez
Jose Ramon Perez
Zoila Perez-Chanquet
Lucia Perez-James
Jeff Perrin
J. Perry
James Perry
Jeff Perry
Larry Perryman
David Persky
Cal Peters
Joan Peters
Cynthia Peterson
Floyd Peterson
Pura Petrillo
Stanka Petrovich
W. Fred Petty
Summer Pfeiffer
Elisabeth Pflaume
Brain Phillips
Jeanette Phillips
Randall Phillips
Stephen Phillips
Tom Phillips
Debbie Phillis
David Phipps
Jennifer Phipps
Eugene Picciano
Oscar Pichardo
Donna Pickard
Vern Pickup-Crawford
Ana Piedra
Rachel Piering
Thomas Piero
Margie Pikarsky
Ronald Pilenzo
Pat Pillmore
Leonides Pimienta
Thomas Pina
Juan Pineda
Sergio Piniero
Clotilde Pino
Julio Pino
Harry Piper
Tony Pistone
Deborah Platt
Nick Pocengal
Daniel Poirot
Juan Polanco
Michael Polemeni

Marcia Pomares
George Poncy
Elaine Pons
Deana Poole
Eric Poole
Lisa Portelli
Jan Porter
Mercedes Pose
Stanley Posey
Kent Postlethwaite
Ronald Postma
Michael Potaczala
Jeff Potter
Robyn Potter
Judy Potts
Galen Poulin
Douglas Powell
Gary Powers
Geraldine Powers
Ken Powers
Ivan Pozo-Illas
Carol Pratt
Megan Pratt
Steve Precourt
Calixta Prendes
Charley Price
Laurie Price
Julio Priede
Eduardo Prieto
Jesus Prieto
Joaquin Prieto
Annette Primiani
Sibille Pritchard
David Pritchett
Cissy Proctor
Alberto Proenza
Herminia Proenza
Esther Proveyer
Dennis Prucha
Donna Pruett
Richard Puddy
Iris Pulido
Orlando Pulido
Ruben Pupo
Sal Purpura
Lori Pyle
Ruth Qualich
David Quinones
Emelino Quintana
Oscar Quintana
Gisela Rabassa
Sonia Radillo
Paula Raeburn
Diane Raines
David Ralph
Ceferino Ramirez

Orestes Ramon
Terry Ramsey
Lawrence Ranch
Linda Randall
Andrea Rankin
Bobbi Rankin
Tim Ransch
Chris Ranung
Alberto Raphael
Joe Rasco
Tammy Rasmussen
Fran Raszmann
Karl Ratti
Maria Victoria Ravelo-Avila
Sally Rawlins
Jeff Ray
Henn Rebane
Bonnie Redding
Deborah Redditt
James Reed
Barbara Reedy
Myriam Reeves
Karl Reichelt
Brenda Reid
Brittany Reid
Phylisa Reid
Estella Reimer
Robert Reinhagen
James Reiss
David Reiter
Cynthia Rennick
Ron Renuart
Edison Reuben
Keith Revell
Marta Rexach
Carlos Reyes
Robert Reyes
Rose Reyes
Alan Reynolds
Jeanne Reynolds
Alan Rezai
Lou Ricca
Ricky Ricci
Helen Rice-Richard
Donald Rich
Sharon Rich
Lois Richards
Richard Richards
Bob Richardson
Mary Richey
Wanda Richey
Kurt Richter
Bob Rigby
Colleen Riley
Ellison Riley
Eric Riley

L. Riley
Alison Rimer
John Rinehart
Mercedes Rios
J. Ripley
Mike Rippe
Carlos Rippes
John Rispoli
Tamara Rivera
Guillermo Lino Rivero
Felix Rivero
Jose Rivero
Graciela Riveron
Orlando Riveron
Cindy Roach
Cossetta Roberson
Clements Robert
Scott Roberti
Bob Roberts
Carolyn Roberts
John Roberts
William Roberts
Kaye Robertson
Allan Robinson
Brett Robinson
Dale Robinson
Ellen Robinson
Roxanne Robinton
Ana Robledo
Michelle Robleto
Teodina Roca
John Rockwell
Linda Rodgers
Anthony Rodio
Zenaida Rodon
Raymond Rodrigues
Lazara Rodriguez
Marco Rodriguez
Maria Antonia Rodriguez
AF Rodriguez
Alejandro Rodriguez
Argelio Rodriguez
Christine Rodriguez
Consuelo Rodriguez
Encarnacion Rodriguez
Florencia Rodriguez
Jenny Rodriguez
Jose Rodriguez
Laura Rodriguez
Manuel Rodriguez
Marta Rodriguez
Mertelina Rodriguez
Norberto Rodriguez
Pasqual Rodriguez
Rachel Rodriguez
Reneida Rodriguez

Roberto Rodriguez
Zulma Rodriguez
Carmen Rodriguez
Shirley Rogachesky
Annick Rogers
Bonnie Rogers
Ofelia Roic
Maria Rojas
Fredy Rojas
Valerie Rolland
Alfredo Romaguera
Nancy Romani
Lynn Romano
Bea Romans
Dalina Romero
Gloria Romero
Isabel Romero
Lourdes Romero
Luciano Romero
Gloria Romero Roses
Tod Roobin
Jan Rooney
Lucille Rosado
Henry Rose
Becky Rose
Lisa Rose-Mann
Danny Rosemond
Charles Rosenberg
Mark Rosenberg
Paul Rosenberg
Wayne Rosenthal
Alex Ross
Donna Ross
Kingsley Ross
Thomas Ross
Erin Rosskopf
John Rothell
John Rousch
Kristan Joy Rousey
Sharon Rousey
Tiffany Rousseau
Patrick Rowley
Sydney Roy
David Rub
Reno Rubeis
Henry Rubin
Michael Rubin
Martha Ruder
Lynn Rued
Mario Rueda
Richard Ruffing
Bernardo Ruiz
Georgina Ruiz
Mario Ruiz
Mercedes Ruiz
Magoly Ruiz-Calderon

Mary Rumberger
Keith Rupp
Nannette Rupp
Steve Ruprecht
Sandra Rushlow
Preston Russ
Kenneth Russell
Monica Russo
Arthur Rutherford
Darlene Ryan
Marc Ryan
Nancy Ryan
Stephanie Ryan
Frank Ryll Jr.
Pat Sabiston
Caridad Sabrot
Mark Saint-Vincent
Isidro Saiz
Cesar Salas
Adelaida Salgado
Vicente Salgado
Mary Ann Salis
Joyce Salomon
Judith Salpeter
Dan Salvetti
Jennifer Sam
Remzey Samarrai
Tony Sammartino
Avery Sams
Michael San Filippo
Joseph Sanches
Aida Sanchez
Alberto Sanchez
Candido Sanchez
Carlos Sanchez
Fernando Sanchez
Humberto Sanchez
Miguel Sanchez
Olga Sanchez
Ricardo Sanchez
Roberto Sanchez
Rose Sanchez
Elvira Sanchez-Breton
Mario Sanchez-Breton
Harlan Sands
Jason Sanford
Rich Sanford
Denver Sangrey
Jesus Antonio Santana
Aida Santana
Jose Santana
Luis Santana
Benita Santiago
Zenaida Santiz
Richard Santos
Maria Teresa Santos

Deborah Sapp
Gregory Sardoy
Emanuel Sarmiento
Stephenie Sasse
Louis Satriano
China Saugar
Brian Saula
Luis Saumell
Joe Saunders
Michele Saunders
Rusty Saunders
Joe Saviak
Connie Savidge
Leonard Sawyer
Madelyn Saylor
Phillip Scanlan
George Schaefer
Paul Schattner
Andrew Schatz
David Schatz
Eileen Schechtman
Ed Scheiblhofer
Bob Schemel
Al Schiff
David Schindler
Joanie Schirm
Ilona Schmidt
Kathryn Schmidt
Bonnie Schnapier
Harriet Schnepp
Shannyn Schott
Diane Schrier
Chuck Schroeder
Greg Schuckman
Anthony Schueth
Jim Schultz
Bonnie Schulze
Rick Schuster
David Schwartz
Michael Schwartz
Sheldon Schwartz
Charles Scott
John Scott
Martin Scott
Randall Scott
Steve Scully
Brittni Seabrooks
Ruben Sebastian
Jose Secada
Victoria Secada
Kim Sedor
Patrick Sefton
Lewis Seifert
Jamie Self
Robert Seltzer
Irwin Seltzer

James Selway
Elizabeth Seman
Caridad Semino
Mark Sena
Jennifer Seney
Kelly Senft
Joel Sensenig
Carmen Sequeiros
Roman Sequeiros
Julio Sera
Manuel Serantes
Andrew Setty
Suzanne Sewell
Norman Shafer
Chris Shaffer
Pamela Shaffner
Linda Shallenberger
Rita Shannon
Dave Shaver
Cardiff Shea
Jon Shebel
Gabe Sheheane
Julie Sheppard
Kevin Sherin
Joanie Sherm
Cindy Sherwood
Grace Shinell
John Shipley
Mary Shiver
Cathy Shonk
Iliana Shorthouse
Christopher Shoucair
Bob Shrader
John Shreffler
Joanne Shrewsbury
Sandy Shugart
Amy Shuler
Elizabeth Shulman
Larry Shultz
Janice Shytle
Sophia Siciliano
Willard Sievers
Joan Sigal
Steve Sigal
Mary Sikes
Gregory Sikosek
Mary Silva
Anthony Silva
Richard Silverman
Ken Silvestri
Isabel Simeon
Denise Simon
Don Simon
Marianick Simon
Jennifer Simpkins
Donna Sines

Carole Singleton
Paul Sirmons
Ing Siverts
Paul Sladek
Sam Slay
B. Slider
Michael Sloan
Jodie Sluss
Traci Small
Chuck Smeby
Lorraine Smeby
David Smith
Ann Smith
Art Smith
Carol Smith
Curtis Smith
Earle Smith
Greg Smith
James Smith
Jennifer Smith
Jessica Smith
Jim Smith
John Smith
Kerry Smith
Lee Smith
Maria Smith
Nevin Smith
Randall Smith
Sandra Smith
Steven Smith
Susan Smith
Timothy Smith
Venus Smith
Yolanda Smith
Art Smith
T. Smith
Patricia Smolar
Ralph Smyth
Burt Snearly
Bill Snooks
Mike Snyder
Paul Snyder
Francisco Snyder
Ramon Soler
Maria Soler
Ricardo Solis
Claire Solis
Elisabeth Solt
John Sommer
Krista Soriano
Ciro Soroka
Elam Sosa
Lee Sosa
Regina Sotolongo
Rinel Sousa
Scott Spages

Judy Spann
Michael Sparker
Paloma SparrowHawk
Edward Spears
Beverly Speir
Anne Spencer
Amy Speno-Geraci
Rachel Speroni
James Spratt
Jim Spratt Spring
David St.Pierre
Sean Stafford
Helen Stankiewicz
Karen Stanley
Niko Stanzione
Deborah Starkweather
Jarrod Starling
Sherry Starling
Earl Starnes
Nicholas Staszko
Larry Stauber
Gus Stavros
Theresa Steel
Todd Steibly
Albert Stellmach
John Stemberger
Chuck Stenso
Michael Stephanos
Charles Stephens
Brenda Stevens
David Stevens
James Stevens
David Stewart
James Stewart
Robert Stewart
Susanna Stewart
Joe Stich
Debra Stiffler
David Still
Paul Still
Robert Stipe
Melanie Stockwell
Cathey Stoltzfus
Cheryl Stone
Thom Stone
Donna Stork
Marc Storter
Dennis Strickland
Lynn Strindler
Charleen Stringfellow
Richard Stroup
Robin Stuart
John Stublen
Christina Stuckemeyer
Mary Stuller
Timothy Stump

Lawrence Stuppy
Felisa Styron
Jose Suarez
Olga Suarez
Dulce Suarez
Vicente Suarez-Resnick
Rosa Sucro
Larry Sugrañes
Adele Sullenger
Leroy Sullivan
Kathryn Sullivan
Clyde Summer
Scott Summerell
Eddie Summers
Nigel Suttle
Ian Sutton
Syeda Swartz
Michael Sweed
Mike Switzer
Lynn Switzer
Wayne Taff
Robert Talamas
Henry Talboys
Ronald Tap
Marion Tarnow
Bill Tate
Charles Tavernise
Fran Taylor
Carl Taylor
Allen Taylor
Brian Tedder
David Teeple
Manny Tejeda
Howard Tendrich
Janet Ternent
William Ternent
Katrina Tew
Ann Teymorzadeh
Gale Thames
John Thayer
Beth Thibodaux
Elizabeth Thiers
Cherie Thomas
Hunter Thomas
Janie Thomas
Kathleen Thomas
Nancy Thomas
Norman Thomas
Patricia Thomas
Allan Thompson
Jim Thompson
John Thompson
Kimberly Thompson
Lonnie Thompson
Tommy Thompson
Lloyd Thrasher

Ronald Tibbonouski
Vanessa Tillman
Margaret Timmins
Bryan Tina
Troy Tippett
Lynn Tipton
Miguel Tirado
Larry Todd
Yenaro Toea
Theresa Tolle
Michael Tomkiewicz
Carmen Tonarely
Danielle Tooke
Rafael Torras
Octavio Torres
Elsa Torres
Jorge Torres
Raquel Torres
Raul Torres
Carolyn Torrey
James Touhy
Elena Tovey
Diana Townsend
Patricia Townsend
Kathy Tran
Peter Travetti
Jose Antonia Travieso
Randi Trazenfeld
Brian Trehy
Thomas Trento
Bob Troup
Phil Trovillo
Ashley Truelove
Andres Trujillo
Sandra Trusso
Alberto Tse
Gary Tucek
Andy Tuck
David Tucker
Pat Tugas
Juan Tur
John Turcotte
Donald Turnbaugh
Judith Turnbaugh
Brian Turner
Carolyn Turner
Diana Turner
Hugh Turner
Lorena Turner
Dick Tuschick
John Twaddle
Roberto Ubeda
Gerri Ulrich
John Unger
Michael Urbanik
Rosa Urossevich

Angel Urquiola
Shawn Utecht
David Utley
Winona Utterback
George Vakalis
Stan Val
Carlos Valarce
Charles Valarce-Stuart
Arsenio Valdes
Blanca Valdes
Rolando Valdes
Alicia Valdes-Dapena
Carlos Antonio Valdes-Dapena
Janet Valentine
Thomas Martin Valero
Jose Valiente
Eugene Valiverdu
Barbara Vanderwyde
James Vanlaurence
Amber Vann
Esmeralda Varela
Christina Vasilakis
Florentin Vasiliu
Jennifer Vasquez
Beth Vassal
Holly Vath
Luis Vega
Carlos Vega
Eric Vega
Maria Vega
Miguel Vera
Jose Verdeja
Robert Verenna
Charles Vermillion
Kristy Verzaal
Jack Vesey
Paula Via
Angelina Viana
Lilia Viana Banos
Jose Vichot
Angela Vickers
J. Vickers
Maria Vila
Taryn Villani
Ana Villasuso
Eduardo Vineta
John Vizzusi
Robert Voke
Ernest Volonte
Helen Voltz
Conway von Girsewald
Gregory Von Hauselt
Kristin Vondrak
John Voss
Rick Wagner
Dennis Wainright

Karen Walby
Janet Walden
Diana Waldron
E. J. Walicki
Felita Walker
Harold Walker
Garrett Wallace
Kate Wallace
Philip Waller
Buzz Walling
Mark Walsch
Casey Walsh
Joyce Wanish
Dick Ward
Betty Warren
Daniel Waterman
B. P. Waters
Mindy Watkins
Amy Watson
Kevin Watson
Linda Watson
James Watt
Carolyn Watts
A. Watts
John Weatherell
Jim Weaver
Jerome Weaver
Russ Weaver
Gou Webb
Larry Webb
Lynne Webb
Stacey Webb
Steve Webb
Toni Webb
Mark Webster
Terry Weeks
Carol Ann Wehle
Mark Weinberg
Kurt Weinel
Mike Weinstein
Jane Weirich
Josh Weiss
Nancy Welch
Jasen Wells
Patrick Welsh
Kent Wennstrom
Harry Wert
Regina Werth
Bob West
Gary West
T.K. Wetherell
Nora Wetzstein
Jay Wheeler
Karen Whetsell
Gloria Whilby
Eric White

Robert Whitehead
Patsy Whitely
Donna Whiting
Mercedes Whitmarsh
Alvina Whittington
Richard Wiack
William Wiedeman
Sandra Wikle
Mark Wilkinson
Heidi Will
George Williams
Michelle Williams
Nan Williams
Oneika Williams
Rob Williams
Zann Williams
Gordon Williamson
Natalie Williamson
George Willis
Anton Wills
David Wilson
Annamaria Windisch
Billy Windsor,
Graham Winick
Tony Winslow
Herminia Wirth
Paul Wirth
Gayle Wise
Marilyn Wise
John Wiseman
Jerry Woelfel
Robert Wolfe
Dan Wolff
Louis Wolfson
Ed Wood
Keith Wood
Peggy Wood
Donna Woodard
Hudson Woodfin
Loretta Woods
Sharyn Woodton-Durham
Gerald Woodward
Arto Wootley
Cameron Worden
David Worrell
Araceli (Angie) Wright
Brenda Wright
Danaya Wright
David Wright
John Wright
Joseph Wright
Kathleen Wright
Kevin Wright
Marjorie Wright
Sean Wright
Tim Wright

Melissa Wu
Carol Wyatt
John Wyche
Jeff Wykoff
Paula Xanthopoulou
Suzanne Yack
Lew Yago
Jim Yancey
Frank Yanez
Ramon Yaniz
Bobby Yanover
David Yarborough
Theron (Terry) Yawn
Terri Yearicks
Bruce Yelverton
Yooni Yi
Heather Youmans
Mary Young
George Youstra
Sergio Ysern
John Yudin
Randy Zalis
Miguel Zamorano
Ronald Zarn

Index

A++ bill, 12–13
A+ Plan for Education, 2, 8–9, 10fig, 11fig, 12, 13–15, 38
ACT, 41
advanced placement (AP), 11fig
Agency for Health Care Administration, 123, 133, 134
Alabama, 47
Alachua County, 107
A.L.E.C., 168
Amiel, Henri, 131
AP. *See* Advanced Placement
Aristotle, 57
Arizona, 85
Asia, 79
Association of Mayors, 168
Australia, 79

Baker County, 123
Ball State University, 47
Bean, Melissa, 86
Berwick, Donald M., 126
Bowen, Howard, 24–25
Bright Futures Scholarship, 10fig, 14, 26
Broward County, 102, 103, 123, 138
Brucia, Carlee, 64
budget, policy and, 53–56
Bundy, Ted, 67
Bush, George W., 112, 144
Bush, Jeb, 8, 101, 122, 125, 137, 158
business development, 147–49

California, 27, 80, 85, 118
Cannon, Dean, 6
Castle, Barbara, 84
Chicago, Ill., 81
child welfare, 98–100, 101–4
Chomsky, Noam, 36
Churchill, Winston, 106

Clay County, 123
Cleveland, Ohio, 165
College Savings Program, 26
Common Placement Test, 14
Constitution, Florida, amendment of, 60–62
Constitution Revision Commission, 60
cost of living, 5
The Costs of Higher Education (Bowen), 24–25
crime: DNA collection and, 65, 66; felony appeals and, 74–75;
   gang/hate group elimination and, 71–74; identity theft, 86–89;
   pornography and, 67–68; prostitution, 68–69, 70; sexual
   predators, prison sentences of and, 64–66

Denver, Colo., 167
Department of Children and Families, Florida, 101–4
Department of Environmental Protection, 106
Detroit, Mich., 165
Dodd, Christopher, 78
Duval County, 123

Economics Research Associates, 144
economy: business development and, 148; education and, 12,
   13, 20, 22; transportation and, 82–83
Edison Schools, 32
education: A++ bill and, 12–13; A+ Plan for Education, 2, 8–9,
   10fig, 11fig, 38; accountability and, 14, 18, 22; AP and, 11fig;
   career academies and, 13, 20–21, 22, 40–41; charter schools
   and, 9; choice in, 9, 10fig, 21, 36–41; community colleges and,
   10fig, 14, 23–24, 27; competition and, 8, 38, 43; curricular
   reform and, 17, 18–19; dropout rates and, 10fig, 20; economy
   and, 12, 13, 20, 22; FCAT and, 11fig, 13–15, 17–18; Florida
   Legislature and, 22, 24, 26, 30; Florida Supreme Court and, 38;
   graduation rates and, 10fig, 22; higher, 23–28; multi-lingual,
   19; private-public partnerships and, 45–47; reform of public,
   8–13; scholarship programs and, 9, 10fig, 14, 26, 39–40;
   school recognition and, 11fig; spending on, 42–47; teachers
   and principals and, 29–35; technical, 20; virtual schools and, 9,
   40
Educator Accomplished Practices, 33
Einstein, Albert, 29

elderly, identity theft and, 86, 87
employment, education and, 20
energy: alternative sources of, 112–16; efficiency and, 106–9
Energy Efficiency Fund, 108
entertainment industry, 144–46
environment: alternative energy sources and, 112–16; energy
  efficiency and, 106–9; Florida Legislature and, 115; fuel-
  efficient vehicles and, 117–20; permitting and, 110–11
Environmental Protection Agency (EPA), 107, 119

Facebook, 98
family: Department of Children and Families and, 101–4; film
  and entertainment industry and, 144–46; protection of, 98–100
FBI. *See* Federal Bureau of Investigation
FCAT. *See* Florida Comprehensive Assessment Test
Federal Bureau of Investigation (FBI), 71
Federal Natural Catastrophe Reinsurance Fund, 94
Federal Trade Commission (FTC), 87
FGBS. *See* Florida Green Building Standard
film industry, 144–46
Finland, 15
First Generation Matching Grant Program, 26
Florida: business development in, 147–49; child welfare system
  and, 101; child welfare system in, 101–4; constitution of, 60;
  cost of living in, 5; crime in, 64–66, 67–71, 71–73, 74–75;
  education in, 2, 5, 8–28, 29–35, 36–41, 42–47; environment in,
  106–9, 110–11, 112–16, 117–20; family in, 96–97, 98–100,
  101–4; film and entertainment industry in, 144–46; healthcare
  in, 2, 5, 122–25, 126–30, 131–33, 134–37, 138–42; housing in,
  89–94, 96–97, 158–62; litigation in, 163–64; litigation reform
  in, 150–53; national idea bank and, 168–69; national influence
  of, 57–59; politics in, 5; poverty in, 165–67; transportation
  system in, 78–83; university enrollment in, 10fig
Florida Chamber of Commerce, 82
FloridaCompareCare.com, 134–36
Florida Comprehensive Assessment Test (FCAT), 11fig, 13–15,
  17–18
Florida Contraband Act, 70
Florida Department of Environmental Protection, 110
Florida Department of Law Enforcement, 71

Florida Energy Commission, 115–16
Florida Green Building Standard (FGBS), 107–8
Florida Health Information Network, 137
Florida Health Insurance Plan, 140
Florida Health Insurance Study (2004), 139
Florida Healthy Kids, 139
Florida Hurricane Catastrophe Fund, 92
Florida International University, 91–92, 166
Florida KidCare, 140
Florida Legislature: education and, 22, 24, 26, 30; environment and, 115; government spending and, 53–56; healthcare and, 122, 123, 125, 133, 134, 140; housing and, 97; litigation reform and, 151; poverty and, 166; transportation and, 83
Florida Rules of Civil Procedure, 150
Florida Senior Care, 132–33
Florida Student Assistance Grant, 26
Florida Supreme Court: education and, 38; litigation reform and, 151
Florida TaxWatch, 156
Florida Virtual School, 40
Fossella, Vito, 37
Frist, Bill, 138
FTC. *See* Federal Trade Commission

Gainesville Regional Utilities (GRU), 107
Gang Resistance Education and Training (G.R.E.A.T.), 72–73
gangs, 71–74
Georgia, 12
Gerstner, Lois V., 29
Gillmor, Paul, 112, 122
Gingrich, Newt, 72
Gladstone, William, 74
government: citizen initiative process and, 60–62; drivers' license services and, 84–85; spending and, 53–56, 154–57; taxation and, 154–57, 158–62; transportation and, 78–83
G.R.E.A.T. *See* Gang Resistance Education and Training
GRU. *See* Gainesville Regional Utilities

Harlem Children's Zone, 103
hate crimes, 71–74

Hayes, Denis, 117
healthcare: 10/20/Life, 2; accountability in, 138–42; e-prescribing and, 2, 136; in Florida, 5; Florida Legislature and, 122, 123, 125, 133, 134, 140; hospitals, tax support for and, 126–30; long-term, 131–33; Medicaid reform and, 122–25; transparency and, 134–37
HealthFlex, 140
Heritage Foundation, 46, 157
homelessness, 165–67
House Interim Workgroup on Affordable Housing, 97
housing: access to affordable, 96–97; Florida Legislature and, 97; homelessness and, 165–67; homeowners' insurance and, 89–94; hurricane destruction and, 89–94; poverty and, 165–67; taxation and, 158–62
Housing First, 167
Hubbard, Elbert, 110
Hugo, Victor, 168
Humphrey, Hubert, 98

IBM, 29
idea bank, national, 168–69
Illinois, 47
Indiana, 81
Iowa, 57, 58

Jackson, Jesse, 165
Jacksonville Electric Authority (JEA), 107
Jefferson, Thomas, 42, 154
Jessica Lunsford Act ("Jessica's law"), 64, 65
Justice Department, U.S., 65

Kingston, Jack, 150
Koret Task Force, 17, 18, 30, 37

LEED program, 107–8
Lincoln, Abraham, 134
litigation: business, 163–64; frivolous, 150–53
living, cost of, 5
Louisiana, 12
Lunsford, Jessica, 64

Madison, James, 53
Manatee Community College, 23
Manatee County, 22–23
Manatee Technical Institute, 23
Manhattan Institute, 38
Maryland, 118
McBride, Sean, 163
Medicaid, 2, 122–25, 126, 127, 132, 136, 138
Medicare, 126, 132, 138
Miami, Fla., 165
Miami-Dade County, 46, 73, 81, 102, 103, 138
Miami Herald, 165
MSNBC, 67
MySpace, 98–99

NAEP. *See* National Assessment of Educational Progress
Nassau County, 123
National Assessment of Educational Progress (NAEP: "The Nation's Report Card"), 11fig
National Center for Missing and Exploited Children, 99
National Environmental Performance Track Program (NEPT), 111
N.C.S.L., 168
NEPT. *See* National Environmental Performance Track Program
New Hampshire, 57, 58, 59
North Dakota, 85

Office of Program Policy Analysis and Government Accountability, 47
Ohio, 27
Opportunity Scholarship Program (OSP), 38
Oregon, 80
Orlando-Orange County, 81
OSP. *See* Opportunity Scholarship Program

Pataki, George E., 96
Payne, John Howard, 89
Philadelphia, Pa., 167

Phoenix Police Department, 73
policy, budget and, 53–56
politics: crises and, 5–6; in Florida, 5; media and, 5; as proactive, 5–6; as reactive, 5
pornography, 67–68
poverty, 165–67
PPPs. *See* private-public partnerships
Prepaid College Program, 26
private-public partnerships (PPPs): education and, 45–47; transportation and, 79–81
Professional Education Test, 33
prostitution, 68–69, 70
PSAT, 11fig

Reagan, Ronald, 147
Redefining Health Care, 128
Reforming Education in Florida (Koret Task Force), 17, 18, 30, 37
Rubio, Marco, 2–3
Ryder System, Inc., 46

SAG. *See* Screen Actors Guild
San Francisco, Cali., 167
Sansom, Ray, 6
Sarasota County, 107
SAT, 11fig, 41
Save Our Homes, 158–59
SCHIP. *See* State Children's Health Insurance Program
Schrock, Jay, 22–23
Screen Actors Guild (SAG), 246
September 11, 72
Singapore, 12, 14
South America, 79
Southern Poverty Law Center, 71
South Florida, University of, Sarasota/Manatee, 23
South Florida Evaluation and Treatment Center, 129
South Florida State Hospital, 129
STAR (Special Teachers Are Rewarded) Plan, 30
State Children's Health Insurance Program (SCHIP), 139, 140
Strategic Intermodal System, 78
Sumter County, 46

Sunshine State Standards, 14, 17
Supreme Court, U.S., pornography and, 67

Tampa-Hillsborough County, 81
taxation: policy for, 154–57; property, 158–62
Taxation Budget Reform Commission, 60
teachers: funding initiatives and, 34–35; liability protection and,
   34; recruiting, 32–33; training of, 29–32
10/20/Life, 2
Texas, 27, 80
Toronto, Canada, 81
transportation, 78–83
*Transportation Cornerstone Florida: Moving Florida's Economy into the
   21st Century*, 82–83
"Truth in Premium Billing" statement, 93
2+2+2 agreement, 23–24
"2004 Hate Crimes in Florida," 71

unemployment, 25fig
United States, education in, 16fig
United States Green Building Council, 107
United States Interagency Council on Homelessness, 167
U.S. Bureau of Alcohol, Tobacco, Firearms, and Explosives, 73
U.S. Census Bureau, 156, 165
Utt, Ronald D., 45–46

Villages, 46
Virginia, 80
voluntary pre-kindergarten program, 18

Washington, D.C., 80
Wilson, Woodrow, 59
Wittle, Chris, 32
workers' compensation, 141